Filling the Happiness Gap

Filling the Happiness Gap

Will Foster

HAY HOUSE

Carlsbad, California • New York City • London
Sydney • Johannesburg • Vancouver • New Delhi

First published and distributed in the United Kingdom by:
Hay House UK Ltd, Astley House, 33 Notting Hill Gate, London W11 3JQ
Tel: +44 (0)20 3675 2450; Fax: +44 (0)20 3675 2451; www.hayhouse.co.uk

Published and distributed in the United States of America by:
Hay House Inc., PO Box 5100, Carlsbad, CA 92018-5100
Tel: (1) 760 431 7695 or (800) 654 5126; Fax: (1) 760 431 6948 or (800) 650 5115
www.hayhouse.com

Published and distributed in Australia by:
Hay House Australia Ltd, 18/36 Ralph St, Alexandria NSW 2015
Tel: (61) 2 9669 4299; Fax: (61) 2 9669 4144; www.hayhouse.com.au

Published and distributed in India by:
Hay House Publishers India, Muskaan Complex, Plot No.3, B-2,
Vasant Kunj, New Delhi 110 070
Tel: (91) 11 4176 1620; Fax: (91) 11 4176 1630; www.hayhouse.co.in

Distributed in Canada by:
Raincoast Books, 2440 Viking Way, Richmond, B.C. V6V 1N2
Tel: (1) 604 448 7100; Fax: (1) 604 270 7161; www.raincoast.com

The information given in this book should not be treated as a substitute
for professional medical advice; always consult a medical practitioner. Any
use of information in this book is at the reader's discretion and risk. Neither
the author nor the publisher can be held responsible for any loss, claim or
damage arising out of the use, or misuse, of the suggestions made, the
failure to take medical advice or for any material on third party websites.

A catalogue record for this book is available from the British Library.

ISBN: 978-1-78180-944-0

Interior illustrations: Shutterstock

Printed and bound in Great Britain by CPI Group (UK) Ltd, Croydon CR0 4YY

This book is dedicated to Alice and Daisy.
You guys rock my world!

Contents

Contents

What Is the Happiness GAP?

*'When I went to school, they asked me what I
wanted to be when I grew up. I wrote down "happy".
They told me I didn't understand the assignment
and I told them they didn't understand life.'*

JOHN LENNON

Have you ever said (out loud or in your mind): 'Once I have x *in* my life or y *out* of my life, *then* I'll be happy'? If your answer is 'maybe' or 'yes', you've come to the right place. This book is designed to fill your spirit with enough of the good stuff to reframe 'I'll be happy when I have…' to 'I'm happier with now, and excited about what's to come.'

Becoming happier, not happy

A few years ago, as part of a self-prescribed experiment, I started doing gratitude, acceptance and meditation exercises to see if they could help increase my happiness.

I noticed very little change at first. Life was still life: full of ups and downs, stresses and strains. As the motivational coach Brendon Burchard pointed out in a YouTube video I was watching one Tuesday evening – after admitting I needed a boost after a tough day – 'common knowledge doesn't equate to common practice.'

At work, the energy-sapping guy still managed to corner me (despite my innumerable attempts to hide from him in the cleaning cupboard); I still found it aggravating when my train was overdue; and although I was more mindful about trying to remain in control of my emotions, my worries about money, health and relationships were still very real and 'there'.

I asked some of my life-coaching and personal-training clients to try my gratitude, acceptance and being present practices too, and their experience was similar to mine. 'I don't feel all that different, Will,' said one. 'But for reasons I can't describe, I'm *happier*. It feels like something I can't explain in words.'

And *that's* what I passionately want people to shoot for in their emotional wellbeing. As Harvard professor and happiness researcher Tal Ben-Shahar says, we should aim for becoming 'happier' in life, but not necessarily 'happy'.

> *Rather than making 'happy' the goal, I prefer folks try for 'What can I do to become a bit happier?'*

In fact, the word 'happy' leaves a weird taste in my mouth that stems from the 'cherry-on-topness' of what happiness really means in our day-to-day lives. No one can be 'happy' all the time, and I believe that's one of the reasons why self-help gurus get a bad rap from 'non-self-helpies' (those who feel they're far too well developed to need self-help, but invariably leave workshops 'de-scepticized' after realizing how much help we *all* really do need).

You see, 'happy' is an emotion that can come and go as quickly as a fart in a stiff breeze. Someone could feel 'happy' after a workout at the gym, only to come home, have a row with his or her spouse and feel angry – all within the space of an hour. Take said man or woman in this upset state and add some social media-induced 'no one should ever be sad' perfectionism, and we have a recipe for double punishment: a) feel bad, and b) feel bad for feeling bad (as guilt, shame, anger, embarrassment or withdrawal kick in that we have a less than blissful existence).

Aiming for 'happy' is like aiming for being 'confident' or 'contented' – words we use to describe a finished product, a final destination, a black-and-white box that, as far as my research and experience have shown, exists only at the fingertips of Hollywood scriptwriters or the perfectionist culture of social media, which displays the trailer to the movie and rarely the full show.

Uncovering the Happiness GAP

Over the last decade, I've researched the work of hundreds of happiness experts – from ancient Greek philosophers to modern-day positive psychologists –

and conducted almost 10,000 hours of one-on-one life coaching, Neuro-Linguistic Programming (NLP) therapy and personal training sessions with CEOs, mums, athletes and everyone in between. What I discovered is that focusing on the cool stuff in your life, accepting what you can't (and can) control, and becoming more mindful of 'the present' leaves us all feeling a *whole lot* happier.

The 21-day GAP programme I created, and launched on my website, was the brainchild of a) all those years of happiness research, b) personal experience, and c) lots of coffee on a rainy autumnal morning spent pondering a way of melting gratitude, acceptance and living in the 'now' into one happiness-boosting pot. What happened next wasn't something I was expecting.

Online, people responded to the GAP programme in a way I'd not seen before. Comments and 'likes' came pouring through. However, rather than let my thirsty ego run wild with the idea that I'd done something 'special' (other than put an acronym together), I simply declared that I'd get to work on developing the GAP into the most user-friendly happiness-boosting programme possible – and that's what you'll find in this book.

Once I started testing the GAP programme on my clients, the results were profound. Many remarked on how much calmer and happier they felt after completing it. Towards the end of her 21 days, Joanne wrote, 'I'm happier because I now realize what was making me unhappy before.' Her words blew me away, and they sum up why I urge you to give *your* GAP journey everything you have.

The G, A and P in the Happiness GAP programme stand for:

- **Gratitude** for what you have in your life: which helps you realize how cool it is if you slow down enough to notice it; gratitude for the sometimes difficult lessons that life presents to you; and gratitude as a means of helping reduce your stress and view your life from a new and more empowered perspective.

- **Acceptance** of aspects of your current circumstances over which you have *no control* (such as difficult people or lifestyle limitations), which makes for a happier life, despite it not being exactly what you'd planned; acceptance of the things in your life over which you *do have control*: the power to change things if you so wish; and lastly, acceptance of 'what is' in order to release stress, and acceptance of 'what is yet to be' to release inspiration.

- The ability to **be mindful of the Present moment**. This is about becoming aware of the kind of thoughts and feelings you're having in the moment. By growing in consciousness, or 'presence', in this way, you're in an empowered position to allow thoughts to pass through your mind without being affected by them.

A huge part of why I'm so passionate about the Happiness GAP is that it's so easy to remember. And therein lies the secret of its success:

Consistently remembering to practise good happiness habits can help us lead a happier existence.

Like riding a bike, getting started on the GAP does require an initial surge of energy and effort, but once you're up and running, all it takes is a bit of pedalling to keep the wheels moving. Your happiness is much like those wheels, and I believe that's why books like *The Power of Now*, *Don't Sweat the Small Stuff* and *Feel the Fear and Do It Anyway* have made such an impact.

It's not just because they're great books; it's because their titles sum up what we want and need to practise in our daily lives – quickly and easily keeping the wheels of our happiness constantly moving forward.

Stop chasing the butterfly

Before we go into the GAP programme, let's look at where this discontentment with life originates, and how we can overcome it. To me, among the many factors involved, the one that stands out more boldly than any other is the mistaken belief that life can ever be 'perfect', otherwise known as perfectionism. Modern psychologists agree that perfectionism is a 'black-and-white' view of the world – one in which things either work or they don't. There's no middle ground or room for growth.

However, Tal Ben-Shahar suggests that perfectionism isn't all bad. For instance, seeking the 'ideal' situation in our working lives leads to positive traits like drive and ambition, which can result in a sense of deep satisfaction through accomplishment and success. Left unchecked, though, these positive traits can spill into over-thinking every detail, an excessive need for control, and a tendency to create an emotional shield to prevent people from seeing our human vulnerabilities.

So, in a truly vulnerable human existence, full of everyday ups and downs, is becoming 'happier' even achievable? It turns out that it is – very much so. How? By ending our chase with the butterfly! We can chase it all we want, but the likelihood of catching the beautiful little ninja bug is almost zero.

On the other hand, when we stop chasing it and slow down, the butterfly comes flying over and rests gently on our shoulder. You see, it's the pursuit of happiness that usually pushes it away. As my friend and marketing mentor Patti Renner said once in a Skype call – during which I think she could tell I'd been chasing the butterfly too much – 'Will, sometimes in life we've got to slow down to speed up.'

Of course there are times when, through massive perseverance and a bloody good net, we *do* catch the butterfly of happiness. But after a period of time spent basking in the glory of our catch, we resume our normal lives. At this juncture, some of us learn that catching the butterfly is:

1. A huge waste of our emotional wellbeing (when we get what we want, we adapt to it faster than you can say, 'Boy, I thought the view of the ocean described

in the brochure would keep me excited for a lot longer than this.').

2. A lot easier to do when we slow down and allow the butterfly to come rest on our shoulder when we're least expecting it.

How I filled my Happiness GAP

It's for those two reasons that I wrote this book. You see, five years ago, I was caught in a butterfly chase. I developed a skin condition called psoriasis. It itched and it stung, but worst of all, it looked horrid.

I didn't want to be intimate with my wife because I was ashamed of the way I looked. To rub a little salt into the wound, it showed up on my face and on my 'other bits' too. In my darker moments, I'd stare up at the sky and say to God or the Universe or whoever: 'Seriously? You could've chosen my ass…an area no one even sees!'

Each day, I'd head into work wearing a brave face, but deep down, I had a disquieting feeling that was always there, like background static I couldn't shift. For years, I thought that if I could only rid myself of the psoriasis, I'd be happy again.

And then, during a surf trip to Sri Lanka around three years ago, my dreams came true. After five days spent surfing in balmy South Asian waters under a blazing hot sun, the crimson red marks that had caused so much emotional pain turned to a light pink. Boy, was I happy! Almost overnight, I was able to make eye contact with people more easily, and become more intimate with my wife. I spent a few days bouncing around like Tigger on class A drugs.

Then one evening, as I sat joking and laughing with a group in a humid restaurant, a strange sensation hit me in the pit of my stomach. At first, I wondered if it was something the chef had put in the curry. I looked down at the yellowy lentils and plush pink prawns in my hand-carved bowl, and was about to take another mouthful when I felt my stomach drop again. It was like the feeling you get when you suddenly remember you've been asked to make a speech or sit an exam.

The same feeling kept coming, over and over again. Each time it did, I brushed it off as a dodgy stomach and crossed my legs a little tighter inside my board shorts! It affected the whole evening and, as we walked back across the beach to our villa afterwards, my wife could tell that something wasn't right in me.

She was about to speak when I turned to her and said; 'I've realized something. I'm over this (pointing at the skin on my elbows). I'm over it and I know it. I've had this truth before – when I've achieved a lifelong goal or when I've made a certain amount of money – but I've never understood what it means in the context of happiness and life.

'I'm over the fact that the psoriasis has almost gone; I'm over the fact I've been on this tremendous high and now I feel just the same as I did before. It seems that, now I haven't got my skin to absorb me, I've started creating similar feelings about

my job and where we should live. When will this end? It feels as if I'm having a fight with my life.'

As I lay in bed that night, staring up at the mosquito netting, I kept having the same thought, over and over again: Will, you've been on a high, but it's over already. You feel the same as you did before. How can this have happened? Two f***ing days! Is that all? A two-day high for the thing that's caused five years of pain?

I'd experienced what positive psychologists call the 'adaptation effect'. I'd been on a high, and once it wore off I was back to normal. Indeed, researchers who evaluated the levels of happiness and wellbeing of paraplegics and lottery winners six months 'post-incident' reported no discernable difference. Neither the loss of the ability to walk nor the high of being able to buy a huge house lasted long enough to destroy or increase an individual's happiness.

I love that. Not because I want something bad to happen to other people, and not because I don't want good things to happen either. I love it because it sheds light on how futile butterfly-chasing is. Why?

- Because each moment presents a CHOICE (is the glass half full or half empty?).

- Because the only time it will ever be, is NOW (if we can't accept life's imperfections now, then when?).

- Because the only place happiness will ever exist is HERE (no matter what comes your way in life, if you're here, isn't that all you really need?).

Introducing the Happiness GAP 21-day programme

So, how can filling the Happiness GAP help end the chase with the butterfly? Well, first I want to offer three metaphors that represent how **Gratitude**, **Acceptance** and **Being Present** can benefit your mind, body and soul.

Gratitude is like a muscle

When we lift weights, the muscles and tendons surrounding our joints get stronger, making us more resilient to the rough-and-tumble of everyday life. In much the same way, practising gratitude for all that you have in your life on a regular basis strengthens what I call the 'gratitude muscle'.

Each new thought or feeling or action of gratitude creates new neurological pathways in your brain that make it easier for you to see the positives in life, despite the inevitable curveballs it throws at you. Very few people are 'positive' without having made the effort to be so – in the same way that very few of us have toned buttocks without performing lunges (and no, the machine that wiggles your ass side-to-side for you doesn't count).

When Anna goes to sleep with the lullaby of how cool it was to receive a heartfelt compliment from the lady who served her coffee that morning – rather than dwelling on what a naysayer her mother-in-law was when she told her to forget her dream of living in the mountains one day – it seals her day with a kiss.

Is it a kiss that denies the reality of our everyday stressors and problems? No. Is it a kiss that fills our spirit with enough resilience to help deal with the s*** that's thrown at us on a daily basis? Yes.

Regular gratitude work is like going to a gym for your happiness. Which is why in the Happiness GAP programme you'll be completing a variety of 'gratitude strength-training' exercises.

Acceptance is like a free-flowing river

Imagine that your thoughts and feelings are flowing down a river, like water. Each time you attempt to stop/banish a thought or a feeling, you create a build-up of water (negative energy) that causes a blockage in your 'emotional river'. However, if you instead choose to accept your thoughts and feelings for what they are – perfectly normal and human – the blockages are cleared and the river runs freely once more.

Take Zoe, one of my clients. She put on a good front to the world, in the form of a bubbly and happy personality, but battled internally with negative self-chatter related to being single. And, deep down, wanting to meet someone one day. After taking the GAP programme, Zoe realized that it wasn't the thoughts about being single or a little overweight that got to her, but the fight to *suppress* those thoughts.

For years, Zoe was ashamed and angry at having those negative thoughts about herself, which created a blockage in her emotional river. However, once she understood the need to acknowledge and *accept* her true thoughts and feelings, they passed more quickly. This inspired her to take a new path towards what she really wanted.

The GAP programme features a series of acceptance exercises designed to keep your emotional river flowing, and clear any blockages.

Being present is like surfing

Living in the present moment is like surfing a wave with calmness, confidence and skill. You'll recognize a good surfer – he knows that if he's to harness a wave's power and ride to shore, he must remain present with the ebb and flow, relax, and respond to what the wave is doing in any given second. If the wave slows down, he surfs back to where the power is – the breaking part of the wave. He's reacting to what's happening in the present.

The 'un-conscious surfer' pumps his board across the slower part of the wave, losing all flow (and blaming the wave for his inadequate ride). The conscious 'present-moment surfer' is out there to have fun and be in the moment; she never blames the wave – she knows that Mother Nature is in control, so all she can do is have faith in her ability to stay connected and present with what the wave wants to do and just enjoy the ride.

In life, there will be times when you're flying down the line of a blue wall of liquid perfection. Savour every moment. There will also be times when you're moving slowly, perhaps to the point where you feel as if you've stopped. For example, the birth of a first child is a spectacular moment of elation that's very easy to 'be' present with. All of our senses are so 'in the moment' at such times, that all we have to do is relish it.

But how about beyond the spectacular events? How about the mundane day-to-day ones? Or when life throws us unexpected curveballs? What's the key to staying present, even when our mind seems to pump relentlessly across the waves of past memories or future worries?

The answer is the presence exercises in the GAP programme, which will teach you to stay in the moment on any wave that life presents you. As the saying goes, 'Stress arises from being here and wanting to be over there.'

How the Happiness GAP programme works

Before we start to fill *your* Happiness GAP, I want to explain how the programme is designed and how it can help increase your happiness.

It runs for 21 days and is organized into four sections, in each of which you'll find three GAP exercises – one for gratitude, one for acceptance and one for presence;

these sit under 'G', 'A' and 'P' headings respectively. To get the most out of the programme, be sure to complete the exercises set for each section, and don't read any further until you've done so. Keep an open mind and be kind to yourself while doing the exercises. If you slip, no worries. Get back on the horse and practise again until it starts to become a habit. Here's a quick overview of the content of each section:

Days 1–5: Laying the foundations

The first section covers the basics of the GAP programme and its gratitude, acceptance and presence exercises, enabling you to grasp how they work and start practising them right away. In the same way that you wouldn't go for a run without a warm-up and stretches, I wouldn't want you to take on the GAP without first completing this section.

Days 6–10: Putting the Happiness GAP into action

This is where the challenge level goes up a little: I want to get you outside your comfort zone. As the US fitness expert Fred DeVito says, 'If it doesn't challenge you, it doesn't change you.'

During days 6–10, you'll complete gratitude exercises designed to increase self-reflection and vulnerability, and boost your purpose and perspective; these are followed by acceptance exercises that will unblock your emotional river and restore its flow; lastly, deep-breathing meditation exercises will help you ride your day-to-day waves (no matter how big or scary they might be!).

Days 11–15: Bridging the Happiness GAP

By now, you'll be getting more and more used to practising the gratitude, acceptance and presence exercises on a daily basis, so this section is about building on the previous phase and really stapling these positive happiness habits.

Expect more mindfulness 'in action' to calm your senses, more vulnerability from the gratitude exercises, to strengthen feelings of contentment, and more flow in your emotional river created by accepting what you *can* change in your life.

You've almost filled your Happiness GAP and are likely to wanna start hugging people in the street! A word of warning though: not everyone likes hugs from strangers – especially from enlightened souls like you!

Days 16–21: Bringing it all together

This life is never still or static, and neither is this programme or you! This wave is coming to the end of its cycle. But like all energy, it never leaves the Universe. It goes inside you and onwards to your next steps!

During this final stage you may find that things seem to 'click' in a way they haven't before. However, if you don't have any aha moments, don't force them. Allow yourself the room to explore the exercises in your own unique way. Once you've completed the programme, my hope is that you:

1. Appreciate the benefit of having a strong gratitude muscle, a free-flowing emotional river, and the ability to stay in the moment on any wave that life presents you.

2. Begin to understand the ancient Greek philosopher Aristotle's assertion that 'the true art of happiness is balancing present joy with future purpose'.

If you're like me and have the memory of a goldfish, you might want to carry the book around with you over the 21 days, so you can follow each section as it's laid out. For inspiration, throughout the book you'll find real-life case studies of the Happiness GAP in action – including my own experience, and those of some of my coaching clients.

Tips from your coach

Here's some advice for getting the most benefit from the programme:

- **Partner up.** If you're the type who does well in teams or pairs, it might be a good idea to share the action with others – for accountability and motivation.

- **Stay optimistic.** If you're open to the possibility of becoming more fulfilled, satisfied, content and overall happier with life, then you'll get good results (if it's the other way round, you know the rest).

- **Stick with it.** If you notice your motivation dropping or find that other things keep getting in the way, don't fret. As the GAP rolls out, you'll probably find yourself with more time and energy on your hands than you had before. Why? Well, the happier you feel, the more energy and focus you'll have. The more energy and focus you have, the less time you'll need to get things done. Result = more time on your hands to do things you love! It's a win-win!

- **You can't get the benefit without completing the course.** Ali Campbell, my mentor and coach, once said to me: 'If someone wants to see the benefit of something, they've gotta stick the course. It's just like getting prescribed antibiotics by the doctor – if she says keep taking them for 10 days but you only do two, how can you expect to feel the benefit?' Take the truth in Ali's words as you enter this journey, my friend. I have faith in you.

- **Overcoming obstacles.** If you find a particular section difficult, stay with it for a while before you move on to the next.

PART I

The Happiness GAP
21-Day Programme

Laying the Foundations

'The journey is the destination.'

DAN ELDON, PHOTOJOURNALIST

On these first days of your Happiness GAP programme, I urge you to keep an open mind. Go into the process to find what you find, rather than with a specific goal, such as to 'sort your life out'. I know that might seem peculiar if your intention was to transform your mind, body and soul in the shortest timeframe possible. It's just that, if you did, you're coming in with a mindset that leaves this programme unable to help.

It's like when people decide to crash diet: there's often positive short-term change from the reduced calorie intake, but the long-term solution – a better mindset around food as a whole – isn't addressed. The GAP programme offers positive short-term change, too, but the real work comes in continuing its gratitude, acceptance and presence practices *for life* (I'll explain how to do this in Part II of the book).

Remember what I said earlier about perfectionism and seeing things in black and white? Well, as you go into the GAP, I want you to be aware of perfectionist tendencies. Rather than seeing things through a 'this will either make me happy or it won't' lens, try looking at them through a 'I'm curious to see what this will bring up for me' lens.

The first lens creates a tremendous amount of pressure for your GAP success, which could lead to pessimism if the exercises don't work for you. However, if you adopt the second lens, you're more likely to use the GAP in much the same way you'd hire a sherpa in order to climb a mountain. You still have to do the work, but the sherpa (the GAP) is there to assist your journey and steer you in the right direction.

Happiness fluctuates

Before we begin, I think it's important to note that our happiness levels can fluctuate, in different ways at different times, depending on what's happening in our lives. For example, imagine you have a project that needs to be completed in two weeks' time. You might go through a period in which *pleasure is reduced* through lack of spare time to pursue your hobbies, but *satisfaction is increased* through winning the daily battle with productivity.

Or you might start a blog aimed at improving people's health; this would *increase your sense of purpose* but *reduce your contentment* with the present, as frustrations arise when the blog isn't a success at first.

The point I'm making is that our happiness levels tend to fluctuate with the changing seasons of our lives. However, although our *outer* lives fluctuate, the one thing that's constant throughout is our *inner* world: the way we perceive things. Do we see the glass as half full or half empty?

Do we allow the late train to aggravate us or do we let it go and embrace the moment instead? Do we let that nagging feeling that our life lacks depth and purpose get to us, or do we summon the courage to fulfil our creative destiny?

It's true that our outer life affects our happiness, but according to research, only by as little as 10 per cent. And that's where the Happiness GAP comes in: the remainder depends on how we *see* our world.

Right, one last thing. For your Happiness GAP journey, you'll need a journal in which to complete the exercises, and note your insights and scores. Oh, and a pen!

P – Bring your awareness to the present

Your first challenge is to do a 10-minute meditation *every morning* for the next five days:

Presence exercise

1. Immediately after waking (and visiting the bathroom!), sit on the edge of your bed and set the timer on your phone to 10 minutes.

2. Close your eyes, and bring your attention to the present moment by focusing on your breathing. Take deep breaths, in through your nose and out through your mouth; inhale for roughly four seconds and exhale for roughly four seconds.

3. Each time your mind drifts off to other things, bring your attention back to 'now', and to your breath. The wave you've woken with is the one you're on, so don't try to be off on another. Pay attention to allowing what's happening in each second to happen, without trying to change it.

Tips from your coach

Here's some advice for getting the best from the 10-minute morning meditation.

-   If you have a headache, a 'thing' going on with your partner, a problem at work, a niggle in your body – anything negative – don't wish you didn't have it. Instead, just go with the sensations and allow yourself to *be* with that moment (rather than wanting to force it elsewhere). If you feel wonderful, that's great! Be grateful for feeling what you feel.

- One of my favourite meditation coaches, davidji, has his clients practise the WPM technique, which stands for 'wake-pee-meditate'. I swear by this little lifestyle hack. It's about not letting anything interrupt what I believe is the most important happiness and wellbeing practice of all. Just don't get the order wrong!

- Don't worry if your thoughts really drift and you notice you haven't been focusing on your breath for a while. It happens. You'll get better at it.

- Go in with an open mind and 'no goals'. The moment you see meditation as your 'saviour', you turn it into something that can never do that for you. As davidji says, 'you go in to find what you find'.

- The 10-minute morning meditation is the most important thing to do in these first five days of the GAP programme. Set the timer on your phone, and get it in. Don't fret if you feel you're not 'good' at meditation; in fact, you can't be 'bad' at it. It's true that you can achieve perfect, thought-free bliss, but only after *years* of practice. Initially, just notice what you notice, and whenever your thoughts drift away from focusing on your breath, gently bring them back.

A – Accept what you cannot control

Throughout days 1–5, become more aware of your 'emotional river' by doing the following.

Acceptance exercise

Notice if there's anything blocking the flow of your emotional river. Are you getting frustrated or angry about things in your life that you can't control?

Each time you notice tension in your mind or body due to frustration with your current reality, mindset or circumstances, simply accept it and leave it be. I'm not suggesting you settle for second best and let your life go into chaos; I'm just urging you to give yourself a release from trying to fix every problem, chore and stressor all at once.

Give yourself a score out of 10 for acceptance each day, either mentally or written down in your journal, with one being 'not very accepting' and 10 being 'fully accepting'; see if you can raise your game as each day passes.

Tips from your coach

Here are two ideas for using acceptance to maintain your emotional flow.

- Push your right and left hands together as hard as you can. Now push harder with your right than your left. Did your left hand automatically resist the right? I'm assuming your answer was 'yes' (unless you have one arm much stronger than the other!). It's this 'resistance' we feel when we get frustrated with the things we can't control.

  The only way to stop fighting with our inner resistance is to stop unconsciously trying to 'force' what can't be changed right now. If your reality dictates x, allow x to be, and you'll notice a subtle but profound shift within.

- Talk to people about your feelings on matters of the heart. Accepting that we all need help is one of the most positive changes we can make towards a happier life. You don't have to bare your entire soul on day 1 if you feel shy or awkward. Just spend a moment reflecting on where you think you stand. If you have a gut feeling that a little help would be a wise move for your emotional flow, then start to open up!

G – What was good about today?

When you head to bed on these first five days, grab your journal and pen, and complete the following exercise to give your gratitude muscle a workout:

Gratitude exercise

Reflect on what you're grateful for in your life.

Now write down all the things that you're thankful for having experienced, had or done that day – anything from how your morning coffee filled you with energy to how blessed you were walking into work with two perfectly functioning legs.

It doesn't matter how big or small it is, all that matters is lying in bed and reflecting on the day's events.

As you did for 'acceptance', each day, give yourself a score out of 10 for gratitude, either mentally or written down in your journal; see if you can raise your game as the days roll out.

Tips from your coach

- Keep your journal and pen right next to your bed. (Having them elsewhere in the house is enough to stop the habitual path-of-least-resistance human in you from getting your tired butt out of bed to go and get them.)

- Think back through your day from the beginning, and pick out positive bits worth noting. Focusing on the positives in your life is like going to a gym for your happiness, but don't be hard on yourself if your gratitude muscle feels a little weak initially. Trust me: it'll get much stronger over the next few weeks!

- If your day has been particularly hard, make a note of what life is teaching you. Did that unfriendly girl or guy show you what kind of human you *don't* want to be? Was overeating on junk food before bedtime a sign you could take better care of your stress levels during the day? Whatever negative things you've experienced during the day, see if you can 'reframe' the picture through a fresh pair of eyes.

Days 1–5 recap

G – Each evening, strengthen your 'gratitude muscle' by recording in your journal the 1–1,000,000 things in your life for which you're grateful.

A – Accept what you can't control, and allow things just to *be*, over and over.

P – Start your day mindfully in the present moment with the 10-minute meditation.

Days 1–5 reflections

Answer the following questions, either mentally or by writing them down. Don't ponder them for too long – just go with your gut and see what comes up for you.

▶   Which three things did you learn about yourself, your thinking, your habits and your lifestyle in this first section of the GAP programme?

▶   Which three things might you want to improve on during the next section?

Putting the Happiness GAP into Action

'Yesterday I was clever so I wanted to change the world. Today I am wise, so I am changing my self.'

Rumi

G – Who are you thankful for?

Over the next five days, I'd like you to continue with the gratitude journaling before bedtime, and also complete the following gratitude strength-training exercise.

Gratitude exercise

Each morning, write and send a text message to one person, telling them what they mean to you and why.

The challenge is to be as open as you can be to these five people (one per day) – don't hold back on expressing what you truly want to say to them. Be vulnerable, and let them know what they've done or do for you. This is your chance to really make a difference to their day (and yours too!).

Tips from your coach

Here's some advice for writing your messages of gratitude to others.

- If you're feeling a little scared or awkward about writing your text messages, remember the words of the ancient Chinese philosopher Lao Tzu: 'There is no illusion greater than fear.' The moment you hit 'send', all the fear you had around writing a message, and deciding whether or not to send it, will dissipate. That's not to say feelings of uncertainty won't come up relating to how it's received. But that's not the objective of the exercise: the objective is to get *you* to open up.

  If your message is one that would fill your heart with warmth if *you* received it, don't hesitate to send it. And in case you're thinking *Well, no one ever sends me this kind of message, so why should I bother?* you need to remember why you're doing this exercise. It's not because you expect anything in return (although that would always be gratefully received). It's because you want the soul-felt lift that comes from doing something nice for someone else.

- When you review each message before sending it, ask yourself whether there's anything else you could add as a PS. Don't leave *anything* out.

- Know your fruit! If the recipient is like a peach – soft on the outside and soft on the inside – send them as fruity a message as you like! But if they're like a coconut – hard on the outside and medium to firm on the inside – send them a solid message, one that matches the kind of fruit-onality they are.

  However, if you have a gut feeling that your coconut recipient would like to be more peach-like, send them a peach-like message. You won't regret it! It could transform their entire day, month or year.

A – Can you accept other people?

Firstly, each evening after you've written your bedtime gratitude journal, I'd like you to complete the following exercise from life coach Michael Neill's book *Effortless Success*.

Acceptance exercise

1. Think of a person in your past who hurt you for whatever reason, or someone in your present with whom you're experiencing difficulties.

2. Write a short letter to that person expressing *everything* you'd like to say to them – the good, the bad and the ugly. Don't hold back from saying what you'd like to. Be as honest and vulnerable as you can.

3. You can write to the same person each night or five different people over the five days. The letters don't have to be long; they just need to contain *all* the things you'd like to say to *those* people in your life (past or present). In case you leave anything out, include room for a PS and a PPS.

4. Stash your letters in a secret spot so you can go back to them in times of need.

What does this exercise have to do with acceptance? Well, so often, we're completely unaware of how much emotional blockage we create around other people, in the form of the thoughts and feelings we have around the memories of them during our day-to-day lives.

It's only when we put into words what we're thinking in our heads that we're able to accept that they are just thoughts and don't have power over us unless we allow it. Writing 'the letter' puts your thoughts into words, and unblocks your emotional river.

Tips from your coach

- *Don't post your letters!* During one of my seminars, a chap raised his hand and asked, 'Will, I really love this exercise, but I have one problem – I'm really scared of sending my letter! Is that normal?'

  'Don't send the letter, pal – unless you have a death wish!' I replied. Don't let me stop you from sending *your* letters if you want to, though. Personally, I'd rather come out alive from my next family get-together!

- Make sure the place you hide your letters is genuinely secret! You don't want person x stumbling on their letter while rummaging through your car's glove compartment!

- As a twist, you could choose to write the letter to yourself – I did this recently and the results were really cathartic.

- If you can't think of enough people to write to, send me an email and you can have one of the five I can think of from the 1960s!

Secondly, throughout the next five days, I also want you to 'let other people be right' by doing the following:

Acceptance exercise

If you encounter someone who has a different way of seeing the world, let them say what they need to, *without contesting it.*

Sometimes, it can be hard watching people live the way they do (especially if you're empowered with information that *could* help them). But truth be told, speaking out of turn makes you the one 'with' the information and them the one 'without' it. It's only the ego that wants to be 'right'. Aside from extreme situations, your soul doesn't understand judgement – all it wants is peace.

Tips from your coach

Here are some ideas for 'letting other people be right':

*   If you find yourself in a situation where you want to speak up to contest what someone's said, just be with your thoughts instead. In the split second before you're about to voice what you want to say, ask yourself this easy to remember question: 'Why am I about to speak up?'

    The pause alone should raise your self-awareness enough to help you realize that what you're about to say is coming from a position of 'wanting to be right' – as opposed to wanting to get your viewpoint across to a human who will see it as a form of attack.

- Love yourself enough to want to remain in peace and you'll make the call. I'm not suggesting you don't speak up if there's something you really need to discuss with someone. I'm just urging you to see what happens when you let all those petty, silly, pointlessly stressful conversations just slide by.

~~~~~~~

P – Meditate in chunks

Before we move on to the next stage in your 'mindfulness' training, I want you to continue with the 10-minute morning meditation you began during days 1–5. Ready for the next level?

For years in my coaching practice, I would try to get people to meditate for 20 minutes in the morning before work. However, despite their good intentions, most people failed to make the habit stick. I had that problem too, and therefore ended up not only battling with a worrisome, erratic mind, but also beating myself up for not being disciplined enough to prevent it!

It wasn't until I said 'Ten minutes in the morning will be fine, and I'll see what I can do in two minutes throughout the day' that things began to change.

Maybe you've managed to nail 20–40 minutes of daily meditation (if so, do send me your email – I'd love some coaching!). But if you're like me and prefer to break things up a little, a 10-minute morning meditation followed by bite-sized 'mini-meds' done throughout the day could work for you.

A 'mini-med' is a two-minute meditation. After hundreds of experiments with clients, I've found that two minutes has the optimal ratio of 'Will this actually do anything to help me?' to 'Can I realistically fit this into my day?'

Presence exercise

Your challenge over the next five days is to get one to three mini-meds in per day; here's how:

1. Set the timer on your phone to two minutes.

2. Close your eyes and slow your breathing. Take four seconds to inhale through your nose and four seconds to exhale through your mouth. Feel calm energy enter your body with each in-breath, and tension leaving your body on the out-breath.

3. Throughout the mini-med, focus as much of your attention as possible on the sound and feel of your breath.

Tips from your coach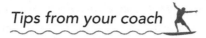

Here's some additional advice for mini-meding:

- Set reminders on your phone to prompt you to do your mini-med. If you get two minutes in the morning before the kids wake up, set your reminder for that time. If you don't get two minutes spare until they've gone to school, set your reminder for then. Just fit it in around your schedule. If you only manage one mini-med a day instead of three, don't fret. That's still good enough to get the benefits.

- If your mind wanders off to the crusty pan you have to wash up ('soaking it' is the single best washing-up deviation tactic ever invented, by the way), bring your thoughts back to the calming sensation of deep breaths. Over and over, bring your attention back to your breath and the present for those sacred two minutes.

- If you find your thoughts move in very scattered directions and at a fast speed, you'll benefit greatly from what yogis call *trataka* – a technique in which you focus intensely on a single object while performing your breathing. It's believed to improve mental concentration and resolve by helping cancel out much of the noise we put up with inside our mind, as well as the outside world.

I use *trataka* daily when performing my morning mini-med session, and it does wonders for slowing down my thoughts. The positive difference with practising *trataka* hasn't been whether I produce negative or irrational thoughts, but more that when they enter my head, they seem to come at a much slower pace, which makes it far easier to let them pass in their own time.

- If you don't get the time to mini-med, do you get time to take a poo? We often forget how sacred a moment that time is – no one to disturb you and ask you to do anything. However (and it's a biggie), taking deep breaths in through your nostrils in that time might come with its own unique challenge!

Days 6–10 recap

G – Send five gratitude text messages, one per day. Be vulnerable. Be open. Make your recipient's day and it will make yours.

A – Write (but don't send!) 'the letter' to between one and five people (or even yourself).

P – Do one to three mini-meds throughout the day. Try *trataka* for slowing down your thoughts, and if you can't set aside time to mini-med, do it while sitting on the loo.

Days 6–10 reflections

Answer the following questions, either mentally, or by writing them down. Don't ponder them for too long – just go with your gut and see what comes up for you.

▶ How did you find the exercises in this section of the programme?

▶ Which three things did you learn about yourself and life while completing them?

▶ How could you take those three things with you into the next section, and the rest of your life?

Happiness GAP case study

Mark (fed up with his mother-in-law, and happier)

Mark and I began working together because he wanted to regain control over his stress levels. He was finding his job as a computer programmer tough going. He was up early in the morning, went to bed late and lived on microwave meals.

He'd say things like: 'My life's a f***ing joke. You wouldn't believe what I have to put up with at work, and then, to make things worse, my mother-in-law is breaking my balls! The other day, she told me she was unsure whether I was fit to be the father of her grandchildren…I mean, seriously! Who says that?'

To be frank, most of our sessions saw Mark hurling as many F-words about his life as he could manage in one hour. And, needless to say, he didn't welcome the Happiness GAP programme with open arms; he ummed and ahhed about it for months, until I gave up trying to help him.

Then, a year into our time together, I told Mark that unless we made some inroads into his development, I couldn't coach him any longer; it wasn't doing my health any good, let alone his. So he agreed to give the gratitude journaling a try. I began by asking him what he was grateful for in his mother-in-law.

'Are you f***ing kidding?' he replied. 'She's a total bitch! What are you on about, grateful for? Is this a joke?'

'No, seriously,' I continued, 'have a think about it. You don't have to like her, just say one thing you can be grateful for in her. You have to spend time in her company, and as far as I'm aware, she's helped you a lot with your business, hasn't she?'

'Yeah, I suppose the financial support she gave me at the start of my business is something to be grateful for,' Mark admitted.

I set Mark the challenge of strengthening his gratitude muscle and seeing how it could help his relationship with his mum-in-law. After 30 days, he reported back, saying, 'I still dislike the woman, but without a doubt, I've noticed how much easier it is to accept her for the way she is. I let her be how she is, without getting into arguments with her. I guess I'm more chilled in a way.'

Mark's experience shows us the power gratitude has to help us accept. Prior to taking the Happiness GAP programme, being 'right' was one of the biggest blockages in Mark's emotional river. He couldn't just accept what his mother-in-law said – instead, he had to make her know that she was 'wrong'. This led to bickering over things as small and silly as which news station had the most reliable weather forecast.

By simply practising a bit of gratitude each evening and allowing his mother-in-law to 'be', Mark was happier about life.

The GAP in action

G: *Mark's gratitude journaling enabled him to focus on who his mother-in-law is (and not so much on who she isn't). Over time, this strengthened the synapses in his brain, wiring new neurological pathways that made it easier for him to see the positives in his mother-in-law, which in turn made it easier for him to be around her.*

A: *Focusing on his mother-in-law's good points helped Mark accept the differences he had with her.*

P: *Mark didn't tell me whether he tried the meditation exercises. He was a stressed-out bloke who would probably have benefitted from them in many ways, but a) it's never my place to force anything on anyone and b) Mark's experience shows us the powerful wave of peace that arrives when we accept the need to 'let others be right' (myself included!).*

Bridging the Happiness GAP

'Consciousness is our only reprieve from time.'

MASON COOLEY, WRITER

Now that you're really making progress, let's move on to seeing how you can step it up a level. In the last section, rather than sitting back and learning the principles, you got in the ring and, before we go any further, let me say how proud and happy I am that you did! The further you progress through this programme, the more challenging it becomes.

However, if you calculate the time it takes to complete the exercises in the coming section, you're looking at just 10–12 minutes per day. And if your motivation ever wanes, remember why you're doing this – to transform your life and happiness.

As Aristotle pointed out so beautifully all those centuries ago: 'Happiness is the meaning and purpose of life, the whole aim and end of human existence.' So, take a deep breath, feel the awesomeness that's coming your way and keep going!

G – Be openly grateful to someone

Firstly, continue writing your gratitude journal each evening and really explore new boundaries of your psyche. Are there areas, people, situations, memories, encounters, feelings, foods, events, sights and sensations you could record that you haven't in the previous sections? The more you explore your mind (and memory) the better it will become at seeing more of the unique and subtle beauties the following day.

Secondly, at some point over the next five days, I'd like you to be openly thankful to a few selected people in your life in a face-to-face meeting. This is a step up from the text message exercise you did during days 6–10 and it requires you to get a little vulnerable.

Gratitude exercise

1. Think of three to five people you could speak with face to face in order to tell them what they mean to you and why. It can be anyone: a friend, co-worker, spouse, client, or the person who sells you your morning coffee.

2. Choose one person to speak to each day. Tell them how much you appreciate their emotional support,

great company, repeat business, help with sorting your finances, ability to make you laugh, glorious talent for lifting your spirits, and so on.

3. There's no need to fear anyone's reaction. There isn't a single human on this Earth who doesn't want to be reminded of their worth and value. Unless you get one of those people who doesn't like being given a compliment. In which case, accept that you can't make a positive impact on *everyone's* life.

And by the way, if no. 3 is you, *accept* the compliment! There's a fine line between humility and self-deprecation and simply blocking a cool opportunity to raise the self-esteem of the person who gave you a compliment and your own. Connection is what our species wants more than anything in this 21st-century life and nothing has the potential to connect us more than wholeheartedly *accepting* 'thank you'.

Tips from your coach

Here's some advice for completing the third gratitude strength-training exercise.

•   While you're selecting people to talk to, consider those with whom you'd like to improve your rapport.

Is there a family member you've found it difficult to get along with in the past, but who ultimately, has provided you with a lot? Let go of the *Well, he/she does or doesn't do that, so why should I do this?* mentality. Remember, you're doing this for the growth of your soul and not your ego. Let it go at the door and be the badass-kindness ninja you know you can be!

- If it's appropriate to have a particular face-to-face meeting in the daytime (because it's with someone at work, for instance), then make this exercise your daytime one. Do it the other way around if evenings are better (for example, if you only get to see the person after work). Fit it into your schedule.

- It's fine to rehearse what you're going to say before you say it, and there's also nothing wrong with keeping things light-hearted. It's just that, if you feel there's something deeper you want to say, be vulnerable!

American social science researcher Brené Brown says it's in our ability to be vulnerable that we humans experience our biggest personal growth and connection. As she suggests in her awesome book *Daring Greatly*: 'Dare greatly, and ye shall be rewarded'.

A – What's blocking your emotional river?

Next, we're going to use a technique called 'reframing' to look at the negative things in your life and spin them into a positive meaning, teaching or lesson you can take with you in the rucksack of your life journey.

Acceptance exercise

1. On a piece of paper, make a list of all the people and situations you can think of that you find frustrating, troubling, annoying, aggravating or saddening.

2. Go through your list and identify the three items that most negatively affect your happiness. Put a * next to these three.

3. Now here's where I hope it gets fun. For each of your * items, I want you to come up with an affirmation that represents your 'letting go' of trying to control these sources of discontentment in your life. You can use swear words, rhyming words, spiritual-yogi-sounding words, words your role model would use – go with your heart as to what comes up for you.

4. Once you've created your three 'self-acceptance' affirmations, I'd like you to read them each morning and evening for the next five days, until you've memorized them. So it's best to keep the wording simple and easy to remember.

Here are a few self-acceptance affirmations coined by my coaching clients:

Sally, on her curvy shape inherited from an even curvier mum: *I'm OK – and my boobs and bum are A-OK!*

Catherine, on her sometimes emotionally distant husband: *Boy, are you a royal shit sometimes, but I love you anyway.*

Ben, on his idiotic boss: *My state of mind is not in your hands – I'm a dude who will choose his mood.*

A few years back, my personal bugbears were my finances, not being able to live by the coast, and my skin condition. Here are the affirmations I came up with:

On my financial situation: *I choose love and acceptance now because I want to feel good, and I know if I choose to feel good, the ride will be fun and money will come!*

On living in London (and not by the coast): *Although I can't fully comprehend it now, I'm beginning to see why London entered my life when it did.*

On having psoriasis: *Mr P, you still suck. And in a funny kind of way, that's all I need for things to be OK.*

Tips from your coach

Here's some advice for compiling your list of bugbears, and coming up with the three self-acceptance affirmations that will help unblock your emotional river.

- If you've only one or two entries on your list, I'd love some coaching – when are you free? You don't *have* to list *lots* of things. It might be one or two big things for you; however, the chances are, if you're anything like I used to be, you might have a fairly long list!

- Keep your affirmations very close to your heart, and expressive of what would release you most from your discontent. Keep tweaking the wording until they hit the note you're looking for.

- Play with the humour, rhyming and philosophical elements in each one. For example, if the wording feels too heavy, lighten it up a little (and vice versa). As the English writer G. K. Chesterton said, 'It's easy to be heavy: hard to be light.'

- I like to put my affirmations up in the bathroom, as a constant reminder of where I want my consciousness to be. But if you'd rather put them on your phone and read them that way, that's fine: it's completely up to you.

P – Become 'super-mindful'

For these five days, I'd like you to continue with the 10-minute morning meditation and the mini-meding one to three times daily. But as you fill your Happiness GAP, let's see how you can 'be present' in as many practical ways as possible.

You see, it's OK for your mind to wander into past memories or future worries during the day. In fact, to remain present for the *entire* day would take a tremendous amount of discipline and skill. So you're not aiming to be *completely* present, just better than you were before. It's *your* journey and the only person you should ever measure yourself against is you.

Below are some 'super-mindful' exercises I'd like you to incorporate into your days during this phase of the programme. See which ones you're drawn to. If one or two seem like the most fun of the lot, go with those. The motivation to do these is calm, but if the incentive involves chocolate, most of us don't need a second nudge (especially dark chocolate with sea salt! OMG, that stuff is lethal!).

Presence exercises

Become 'super-mindful' while doing the following activities:

1. Drinking coffee or tea

Pay closer attention to how your morning/afternoon coffee or tea smells, looks, tastes – its subtle qualities. How does it make you feel? I want you to *really be* with your caffeinated moment, as if it's the last you'll ever have. If you're in a spot where you can watch nature or people as you enjoy your sacred moment, even better.

2. Eating chocolate

Get yourself into a comfortable position with your head supported. Set the timer on your phone for two minutes, then rest a square of your favourite chocolate on your tongue and see if you can make it last the whole time.

Each time your mind wanders off, bring it back to the sensation of the chocolate on your tongue. Inhale for four seconds through your nose and exhale for four seconds through your mouth as you let the sweet, bitter, sour, tangy, nutty, coffee-like notes caress your palate and sooth your soul. If you want to make this one of your mini-meds for the day, go for it!

3. Walking

Try a 'super-mindful' walk. As you take steps, pay attention to your feet as your heels strike the ground, and the feel of your body as it moves forward. See if you can notice things you might not have spotted before. I enjoy looking up high at buildings to see what's going on above my usual eyeline – it seems to spark my consciousness in an 'Ooh, I never noticed that before' kind of way.

Think about how you could bring some novelty and intrigue to your walks. Could you take a slightly different route to work? Or observe things like birds nesting under the roofs of buildings? See if you can add a bit of awe and wonder to it all.

Even as little as 10 minutes of super-mindful walking can release the burden of stress and tension we sometimes feel before a busy day ahead. Try to walk more slowly than you normally would for those 10 minutes. Act as if you have all the time in the world, and in a funny kind of way, you probably will.

4. Eating meals

My sister came up with a wonderful tip for 'super-mindful' eating – put your knife and fork down between mouthfuls. It changes the way you approach each morsel, turning *I wonder how many calories are in this?* into *This cheese is wonderful.*

As an aside, I'm not fussed about whether being present with food helps people lose weight, and that's not because I don't *want* people to lose weight. It's because staying in shape becomes the natural side effect of bringing guilt-free happiness to food.

If you have a slice of chocolate cake, savour it and enjoy every mouthful. Smile, breathe and close your eyes as the gooey texture and sweet taste ease the tension throughout your mind, body and soul. Notice how you *feel* after a treat, too. Does it leave you feeling happy because you've been uplifted by the pleasure? Or unhappy because you now feel guilty?

If you tend to slip towards the latter, bring yourself back to the moment. Each time your mind tries to wander back to regret, bring it back to now. What's been has gone and all that remains is each moment.

Be mindfully present with the joy of eating healthier foods, instead of wishing you were eating richer ones; and likewise, be present with the gorgeousness of richer grub, instead of wishing you could be stricter about eating healthier stuff.

In these five days, you'll start to see why it's the *joie de vivre* the French bring to their food that gives them, on average, the best health and longevity of any country in the world (the average life expectancy worldwide is 71, but in France, it's 88!).

5. Before reaching for your mobile phone or tablet

I love modern technology and believe that, overall, smartphones and tablets have aided our happiness, enabling everything from closer contact with loved ones on the other side of the world, to men and women being able to explore their sexual fantasies without having to sit through the world's most awkward breakfast the morning after a drunken foursome with the neighbours. (Disclaimer: I'm only *imagining* that would be awkward.)

It's just that with tech, as with most things, there's a fine line between it being a really good thing and something we become overly attached to. A good way to notice if you've become dependent on the distraction of your tablet or phone is to challenge yourself to a 'media fast'.

Could you leave your device behind in the car before walking in nature? Or put it on flight mode when you sit to watch a movie in the evening? It's about knowing yourself. Have you ever had a break from it to see how it makes you feel?

Stay very close to your intuition on this one, and over the next five days, see how much media fasting you can do. As an experiment, start with the flight mode for a couple of hours, and I think you'll be pleasantly surprised by what happens.

During a family breakfast last year, my mum-in-law said, 'We did just fine without phones. I don't understand the obsession with them – it doesn't do your insecurities any good.' And, aside from the benefits of increased connection, productivity, laughter and love that can come from modern tech, there's a truth in her words.

I think it's just about finding our individual formula for 'device happiness'. Over these next five days, see if you can find yours.

Days 11–15 recap

G – Be openly thankful in a face-to-face meeting with between three and five people over the next five days. Can you choose someone with whom you'd like to improve your relationship?

A – In which three challenging areas of your life could you consciously remember to practise bringing flow to your emotional river? Create three self-acceptance affirmations, then write them down and put them where you can read them each day.

P – Choose three to five situations in which to become 'super-mindful' over the next five days. Make a note of them on your phone as a reminder, or carry the book around.

Days 11–15 reflections

Answer the following questions, either mentally, or by writing them down. Don't ponder them for too long – just go with your gut and see what comes up for you.

▶ What did you learn about yourself in this section?

▶ If your motivation dipped, could you get a buddy to join in, for the accountability?

▶ Which areas could you improve on?

▶ If you didn't get the most out of a certain exercise, what could you do in the next section to help ease things along?

Happiness GAP case study

Zara (lacking confidence, overweight, and happier)

Zara was a good-humoured lady who came to me for help with her self-esteem and confidence; she also wanted to lose some weight. She trained with me consistently – three times a week for almost seven years – yet it had almost zero impact on the way she looked.

Was Zara's inability to lose weight down to her not changing her eating and lifestyle habits? Probably. I'll never know for sure. Was she happier knowing she was getting the therapy of physical exercise, despite the lack of weight loss? It felt that way to me, until she arrived at a personal training session with a question I'd feared would come out one day: 'Why can't I lose any weight, Will? I'm training all the time but not seeing any results, which feels depressing.'

The rest of our session had a sombre mood. I thought about the accumulation of stress at work and other issues that had led Zara to think, Oh shit! I'm paying to see a trainer three times a week and look at me!

I didn't try to comfort Zara because she wasn't that kind of person. She was a coconut (a hard shell with a softish centre) and didn't need me trying to crack her shell with 'positivity'. I left her to her own devices and accepted her and the situation for what it was. For the next few sessions, Zara did her exercises, complained about her boss, and then headed back to the office.

About a year into my online journey of helping people lead happier lives, Zara arrived at one of our sessions and said, 'You know that gratitude practice you talk about on your Facebook page, Will? I think I could do with something like that – I think I'm too negative sometimes.'

I didn't leap in with a rousing 'Hell, yes! You could really *do with that!' Instead, as calmly and as understatedly as possible, I simply muttered, 'Mmm.'*

Zara had planted the seed of self-awareness, and in the coming weeks, I noticed a softness to her I'd not seen before. She got stuck into the GAP programme, and although she was still very much a coconut, she was turning into a coconut with some give. She reported feeling happier for the following three reasons:

The GAP in action

G: *Zara noticed how relaxing it was to write about her friends each evening in her gratitude journal – the funny things they'd said or nice things they'd done. It helped her go to bed with a feeling of peace she hadn't felt for years, and she slept better.*

A: *She also noticed how much more content she felt when she wasn't constantly trying to change everyone or everything in her life. Each time her boss did something annoying, she repeated her self-acceptance affirmation: 'I ain't gonna take his bait', which made her chuckle and brought some flow to her emotional river.*

P: *Finally, Zara enjoyed her food more. Rather than running through the following day's chores while scoffing ice cream in a guilt-fuelled frenzy, she began to see the wisdom in 'being present' with her Ben & Jerry's Cookie Dough. As she rightly said, 'It's meant to be enjoyable, isn't it? So why not have some damn fun?!'*

Did being present with her ice cream stop Zara from eating the whole tub? No. Did it make her happier to get more pleasure from being mindful of the gorgeousness of a Ben & Jerry's moment? Yes!

Zara's body shape didn't change one bit and, as far as I know, her level of confidence didn't increase that much either. But, as Zara the coconut said, 'I won't do any of your woo woo stuff, Will. But, overall, I can say without doubt that the Happiness GAP has left me much happier.'

Bringing it All Together

*'The key to finding happiness is realizing the only
way to overcome is to transcend; to find happiness in
the simple pleasures, to master the art of just being.'*

BRIANNA WIEST, AUTHOR AND SPEAKER

So you've made it to the final stage of the Happiness GAP programme. During the next six days, we're going to step things up a little from the previous stage. And because of the groundwork you've put in, you'll be ready. Trust me.

So far, your gratitude work has been about other people and things in your life, but this stage is about turning it inwards, and seeing what comes up for you. You see, we're often so good at giving other people credit for what they bring to our lives that we overlook what we bring to the table. For those of you who are low on confidence, the upcoming gratitude exercises may be a real challenge, but remember: *if it doesn't challenge you, it doesn't change you.*

In this section, the acceptance work breaks off into two levels designed to help you create even more flow deep inside your emotional river. Very often, we suppress our emotions, and although we can't consciously acknowledge that this affects our day-to-day lives, in a small way, we'll have that 'blockage' in the form of conversations with things left unsaid, or ambitious creative dreams avoided through fear of failure, and so on.

Lastly, this section introduces the concept of 'flow experiences' – which is doing activities, hobbies or work that leave you wondering where the time went because you were so immersed in the moment. If you already have this positive 'time-less' feeling to much of your day, that's amazing! If you don't, completing the last 'P' in this final section could produce the most profound shift in your happiness of the entire programme!

G – What are you grateful for in yourself?

Firstly, take the following 'self-appreciation' challenge.

Gratitude exercise

1. Send a text message to the three people who are closest to you, asking them what they think are your five greatest strengths.

Is it your baking skills? Our your leadership qualities? Or the fact that others feel more positive after time spent in your company? They'll love to be asked, because they get to be nice; and you'll enjoy being the recipient of their niceness.

2. Make a list of their responses on your mobile phone, or somewhere else you can find them easily. For the next six days, spend a few moments each morning reading through what people are saying about you.

You see, so often, we focus on our weaknesses – on what we should be working on to become better human beings. And before I go any further, I should say I'm *for* that – working on negative habits is something we need to do to live happier lives.

It's just that if you're to fill your Happiness GAP, I want you to reflect on your strengths with a different kind of intention – the kind that motivates you to feel better about the positives you bring to this world and gets you inspired about what the future may hold.

Tips from your coach

- Don't worry if doing this exercise feels a little weird for the first few days. Some of us are so used to talking negatively about ourselves, it can seem strange to give ourselves a pat on the back. The strengths you bring to the table influence all kinds of amazingly positive things.

If you ever doubt that you possess the strengths you see written in your list, treat yourself as you would treat your best friend. Now, maybe you're horrible and would tell your best mate he or she's an idiot, but if you're nice and like to spare people's feelings, picture the two of you together, sitting on a bench. If you doubted yourself, what would your friend say?

Nine times out of 10, he or she will tell you the truth, and the truth is, *you are awesome* – it's only your ego that would ever doubt it. I mean, you don't have to shout your awesomeness from the rooftops (unless you want funny looks). No, no. This is far quieter and more beautiful than that – it's a sacred moment with yourself.

- Tie a strong knot from who you think you might be able to become to the possibility of creating the future of your dreams. There are things you do that no one has ever done like you before; things that no one does like you today, or will ever do like you tomorrow. Your strengths hold the key to the next steps you need to take in areas of your life where you might be feeling stuck.

It's in reminding yourself of your uniqueness, and what you bring to this world, that you will reach new heights of personal growth and happiness. As the 19th-century American essayist Ralph Waldo Emerson put it: 'To be yourself in a world constantly trying to make you into something else is the greatest accomplishment of all.'

- Avoid comparing your strengths to anyone else's! (Unless your comparison motivates and inspires you to achieve more of what they have.)

Take a moment to reflect on what kind of person you've become on your journey so far by ramping up your self-appreciation in the following way.

Gratitude exercise

Complete the sentences below to see what your strengths have helped you achieve and overcome in life.

Here are some personal examples to give you an idea of how this works:

1. I had to call on massive resilience, persistence, patience and courage to become a published author.

2. I learned to be calm and patient to achieve a higher consciousness around money, which has helped me relax and earn more.

3. I didn't know I had so much courage in me – and the ability not to give a shit what people think of my actions – until I healed my psoriasis through naturopathic methods.

I had to call on_____and _____ to become

_____.

I learned to be_____ and _____ to achieve

_____.

I didn't know I had so much _____ and _____ in me until I completed _____ and _____.

A – Put acceptance into action

In the next six days, I want you to see if you can create flow in your emotional river by accepting things on two levels.

Level 1 acceptance is all about bringing a sense of ease and calm to emotions – other people's as well as our own. It's essential that you allow what you *and* others are feeling to be felt. To deny the reality of an emotion is to deny the reality of life itself. If you're to become happier on a deeper level, acceptance of human emotion is a must. Being 'happy' all the time not only denies the reality of being human, it stunts the potential for growth and happiness too. We'll explore level 2 acceptance later.

Level 1 acceptance in action

Let's take a look at some examples of level 1 acceptance to gain insight into how this could work for you. The following scenarios illustrate acceptance of our own emotions *done well* and *poorly*, and acceptance of other people's emotions *done well* and *poorly*.

Acceptance of own emotions done well

My wife turns down my sexual advances. I feel she doesn't care about my needs, and understandably, I'm frustrated. If, in the next few moments, I reject what I'm feeling, I know I'll be denying reality, which will only create an even deeper angst and blockage in the flow of my emotional river.

To accept a situation is to *accept* nature and reality – to understand that in life, crap's gonna turn up sometimes. I decide to feel what I feel *without* rejecting it, and in the end, it takes around 10 minutes for the emotions to pass by naturally.

Having acknowledged the emotions as real and been open to feeling them, I also know that it's something I could change by taking steps to find genuine growth in this area of my relationship with my wife.

Acceptance of own emotions done poorly

My wife turns down my sexual advances, and I feel she doesn't care about my needs. Understandably, I'm hurt and frustrated, but I reject my emotions as 'silly', and block them out with something positive to replace the reality of what I'm feeling.

All this does is distance the real part of me from reality. I'm annoyed at being rejected by my wife, but because I pretend everything's OK, I sweep my emotions under the rug. This results in two negative outcomes:

A. I create a dis-trust between who I *really* am and who I'm *trying to be*, which leads to a drop in self-esteem and confidence.

B. Because I sweep my feelings under the rug, it becomes much harder to get inspired about taking the action step of talking with my wife about our relationship.

Acceptance of others' emotions done well

A friend hurts his ankle while surfing. Understandably, he feels angry at being injured, and I come paddling over to see if he's OK. He's swearing to the high heavens about the pain, and my job is to keep my mouth shut and support him through the process by showing empathy with my tone of voice, facial expressions and body language.

My allowing my friend to feel exactly what he's feeling in that moment enables him to vent his anger and frustration in a healthy way. Sure, his ankle hurts like hell, but the flow I'm creating allows his emotional pain to come pouring out naturally. The result? His ankle is swollen, but emotionally he's exorcised many of the immediate demons we all face when life throws us crap!

Acceptance of others' emotions done poorly

A friend hurts his ankle while surfing. Understandably, he feels angry at being injured. I paddle over and say, 'Oh, you'll be fine, buddy. I saw what happened. You'll be better in no time – you'll see!' Although my remark is well intended, it ends up backfiring because I become the person with the information and he becomes the person without it.

In not letting my friend be with his true emotions, and feel what he authentically feels, I make him resent me and question his own emotional frustration – which only makes him more frustrated. My positivity in the face of negative circumstances doesn't allow him to feel what he wants to feel – the reality of his true feelings. It means he not only feels bad, he also didn't get to express his true emotions because I couldn't accept letting him be right.

Acceptance exercise

In the next six days, your challenge is to put level 1 acceptance into action in what you feel and/or what other people feel. Be *with* your own and others' emotions.

In doing so, I hope you'll begin to notice what it does to get you inspired to make a change that could prevent the thing that caused the pain from showing up again. Which is where level 2 acceptance comes in.

Level 2 acceptance in action

Level 2 acceptance is what the US psychologist Abraham Maslow argued is the highest development a human can undertake: self-actualization. It's about *accepting responsibility* for one's own life and seeking to learn, express creativity and, ultimately, grow.

For the purpose of explaining level 2 acceptance, we can say there are two kinds of mindset in the world: one is closed and the other is open; one is stuck and the other is fluent; one is afraid and unwilling to change, and the other is afraid and willing to change.

It's the difference between having a mindset that says *I don't accept that I'm the one who can control my life path, destiny and happiness, because these are things that are outside my control* versus a mindset that says *I accept that I'm the master of my ship and captain of my soul, and I can decide where I want my life to go.*

One mindset is cowardly, while the other is courageous. For example, an admin assistant has a passion for playing the violin. Staying in her current role and suppressing the nagging feeling she's not becoming who she can become, knocks her self-confidence and self-esteem. If, on the other hand, she accepts the struggle involved in the journey towards her dream, it raises her self-esteem and happiness.

Bottom line: level 2 acceptance is something *most* people aren't willing to embrace, because of the massive challenges involved. The thing those people don't realize is that we don't accumulate happiness from reaching the destination. We get it from accepting it's something our spirit must have to feel truly happy.

Acceptance exercise

What can you accept as being within your control?

If there's an ongoing area in which you're stuck – at work, with your finances, personal relationships, lifestyle, career, or health and fitness – what could you do in the next six days to make a positive change to it?

In your journal or on a piece of paper, write down one area you could work on. Then, alongside this 'goal', come up with three very achievable action steps, like this:

- **Goal:** Improve my relationship with my wife.

- **Action steps:**

    1. Spend an extra two hours of quality time with her each week.

    2. Book the crèche in the gym for 11:30–13:30, so we can work out together and relax in the smoothie bar afterwards.

    3. Give her a spontaneous 10-minute foot rub once a week.

Follow up on your intended action steps and see what comes up for you. My hope is that by taking new, bold and brave action, you'll regain a sense of inspiration for life and what the future may hold.

As I explained earlier, the best reason to set a goal and dream a dream is rarely for the goal/dream itself – rather, it's for the person you're going to become as you journey towards it. It's the feeling of inspiration that will come from stepping outside your comfort zone and growing into the person you know you're capable of becoming.

Adding inspiration to an otherwise happy and contented life is like switching from a Nissan Micra to a Porche 911 for your morning's commute. It won't change the ride from a to b all that much – the scenery will be the same and the local radio station will likely play the same ole tunes – but boy oh boy, it's sure gonna make that ride a whole lot more exhilarating!

P – Have a flow experience

'The hallmark of flow is a feeling of spontaneous joy, even rapture, while performing a task, although flow is also described as a deep focus on nothing but the activity – not even oneself or one's emotions.'

MIHALY CSIKSZENTMIHALYI, PSYCHOLOGIST

For more than two decades Hungarian psychologist Mihaly Csikszentmihalyi studied those states in which people report feelings of concentration and deep enjoyment. His investigations revealed that what makes an experience genuinely satisfying is a state of consciousness called *flow*.

Before I tell you how you can get 'flow experiences' into your life during this phase of the programme, I first want to explain why the ancient Greeks called flow the highest form of human happiness, and what it could do to make a huge impact on your life.

What is flow and how can it boost our happiness?

Flow is characterized by the lack of intellectual thought necessary to achieve it – it's a body/soul experience. When someone's 'in the flow', hours can go by in what feels like minutes, and the result is higher energy, mood and satisfaction. Performing activities that are challenging *and* play to our strengths is the real secret to getting flow in our life.

*Enough challenge + enough strength
to meet the challenge = FLOW*

The best reason for creating the goal of having more flow experiences is simple: you won't have to *think* about whether your life is going in the right direction or not. When you're 'in the flow', you get to feel totally immersed in the present, and any thoughts about where your life feels stuck go out the window.

You see, in many ways, that's the secret to a happier life – not pondering too much on whether you're living one. And that's where the beauty of flow comes in – the absence of our sometimes nagging thoughts. Total immersion in the activities you are doing in the present moment floods the brain with feel-good chemicals, making happiness, confidence and self-esteem things you get without needing a coffee or a glass of wine. It's the default feeling that comes from flow.

A lack of flow, therefore, could be one of the biggest reasons why many people feel unhappy and lacking zest for life. They're too cerebral – too caught up in their own thinking. As the saying goes, 'Don't think too much; you will create a problem that wasn't even there.'

How I found flow

Before we come to the exercise and tips, I want to give you a personal example of how to 'move with' your life so you can always 'find your flow'.

For years, surfing was huge for my happiness because it helped me 'switch off'. Some of you might think that paddling around in waves during the depths of winter sounds hellish, but for me it was (and still is) a timeless heaven.

However, when my wee girl arrived into the world and I started a new career path, the time I got to surf dropped significantly. For a long while, I was much less bubbly than I normally am. It wasn't until I read the work of Tal Ben-Shahar, Harvard University's 'Professor of Happiness', that I realized how much 'flow' surfing had brought me.

I reached a crossroads in my life. Driving for three hours in our boxy van to get to the beach while my wife was in between feeds became unrealistic, and unfair to her. For a good while, I was stuck as to where I could get the flow-based release surfing had given me.

In the end, by following Tal Ben-Shahar's advice and exploring my creative side, I found there was no need to sacrifice my happiness. I didn't know if I'd have enough talent to achieve success as a writer, but other than wanting to help people, my foremost motivation was to achieve more flow experiences in my week.

One paragraph into this book, I knew writing could become my new surfing. When the words I'm stringing together with my fingers meld with the inspirational music playing in my ears, it's a heavenly feeling: one I won't do justice to in describing.

Looking back, I can say that without question, the decision to become a writer has transformed my wellbeing. And the coolest part? Despite the nappy-changing, shopping for groceries, relentlessly keeping our living room tidy enough to walk across, coaching clients and spending time with my wife, I can fit in my writing where and when I like (within reason).

It's free! It's fun! It's uplifting! And it doesn't *have* to create anything more than what it's designed to create:

some awe, some wonder, some curiosity, some sugar and spice to an otherwise normal life.

What about success? Sure, success would be wonderful; I want that for you more than anything, but you don't *have* to use 'outer' motivations as your initial drivers if you don't want to. I found there was a lot less pressure (and therefore a lot more fun) in just exploring the creative/learning/growth process with my mind or body, without trying to second-guess whether people would like what I produced or whether I looked good doing it.

These days, I find that a three-hour writing session can feel like a 20-minute one, and without a seed of doubt in my soul, I believe that if you can find an activity that's easy to access, roughly plays to your strengths, gets you intensely focused and is neither too easy nor too hard, you'll have the key to what the ancient Greeks called *eudemonia*.

Roughly translated, *eudemonia* means 'to be with your positive demon', which, when you experience 'flow', makes perfect sense. It's as if you get taken over by a force greater than yourself; a force that transcends physical and spiritual worlds. A force that I believe, with some perseverance, persistence and patience, you are not only capable of feeling, but are obligated to bring forth to a Universe that wants you to smell, see, hear, taste and feel what it is that ONLY YOU CAN DO IN THE WAY YOU DO IT!

Presence exercise

Spend between five minutes and five hours doing something creative, inspiring and 'flow-generating' on each of the next six days. If it's a brand new hobby, the goal is to get stuck in and not worry too much about the end result – just allow yourself the room to learn, without self-scrutiny.

Tips from your coach

Here's some advice for finding more flow over the next six days:

- You need to start somewhere! The time you spend weighing up which activity to try – should it be painting, sculpture, writing, dancing, acting, public speaking, tennis, stand-up paddle boarding? – could be spent on getting better at reaching flow.

  All you need to know is this: in the beginning, you're probably going to find that you're somewhere between sucky and average at your new activity (and it's your job to be OK with that).

- Remember *why* you're doing this. If you're constantly over-thinking while engaged in the new activity you've taken on, it could be because you're motivating yourself from the outside-in with thoughts like *I'm no good at this* or *I wonder what people think of my moves in this salsa class right now?* Let go of pleasing others or making sure it 'looks' or 'sounds' good – this is your journey into happiness and not your salsa instructor's.

- Be open! If you give something a good try and you still can't seem to grasp the basics of getting some thought-free bliss, keep your mind open to different activities. You don't have to feel defeated just because you couldn't get up on the surfboard the first few times of trying. If something truly defeats you, try something else. Keep exploring new activities until you find one where your natural strengths start to shine through.

- Observe the three pillars of 'pre-flow-clarity' – deep breathing/full hydration/eight hours of sleep, or BHS for short. Let's say you've persevered with an activity (that *does* play to your strengths) but feel you're still not getting thought-free bliss. Well, it's time to work out how you can better produce the right physical state going into the activity.

For example, if I'm feeling sluggish after too few hours of sleep, a bit foggy from dehydration or a little tense from a lack of deep breathing, I find it much harder to reach flow. That's why I urge you to remember BHS. If at least two of the three pillars are taken care of, you'll find yourself in a physical state of pre-flow clarity, making flow much easier to achieve. What if all three pre-flow clarity pillars aren't achieved before you go into your activity? Caffeine! (Need I say more?)

- Keep at it! If you're trying different activities and not quite getting the thought-free bliss of flow, it could be because your skill level hasn't quite allowed your body-soul to take over for you yet. In the process of learning any new skill, your brain and body are busy creating new neurological pathways necessary to 'learn' it. Don't get frustrated with yourself if you're in the early stages. Keep at it and, after some time, you'll see and feel why it was worth the effort!

- Enjoy an awesome side effect of flow: when you pursue your true passion, the Universe will reward you in all kinds of unique ways. The happier you are from getting flow in your day, the easier it will be to manifest amazing people, opportunities and finances to help support your quest that might not have been there before.

If you consider that inner peace and love are the highest possible vibrations in the Universe, when you match what it is you love to do with the feeling of pure peace that comes from doing what you love, before long all kinds of cool things turn up in your life.

As the American anthropologist Joseph Campbell wrote, 'When you follow your bliss, the Universe will open doors where once there were only walls.'

- 'Go with' life! If there's something that used to bring you happiness but you can no longer do it due to lack of health, time, money or confidence, it could be the Universe's way of telling you to seek new horizons.

  For example, if you used to run, but your knee won't allow it any more, could you paint or write poems or play computer games instead? If you think outside the box, there are so many good ways to step out of mind and into spirit. Rather than stay rigid about what could bring you thought-free bliss, become more fluent: learn to 'go with' and you'll be amazed by what's waiting round the corner.

Days 16–21 recap

G – Text three people to ask them what they think are your five greatest strengths. Keep those key strengths in mind as you consider where to take your future. There will *never be another you again!* Remember that before you think of playing this shit small.

A – Let others be right, accept that it's OK to have crappy emotions, and set a goal for an area of your life you could improve, creating three action steps to get there.

P – Bring some flow to your days. The goal is to immerse your body and soul in an activity to such a degree that you forget about your thoughts and about time.

Days 16–21 reflections

Answer the following questions, either mentally, or by writing them down. Don't ponder them for too long – just go with your gut and see what comes up for you.

▶ What did you discover about yourself in this final section?

▶ Which areas could you improve on?

Happiness GAP case study

Stewart (anxious, and happier)

Stewart came to me for help with what he called 'a super annoying, nagging monkey mind – always telling me there's something to be worried about'. One of those lovely people with the heart of a lion, Stewart was very strong for his family and worked hard in his job as a police officer. However, as our time together rolled out, I was fortunate enough to see his vulnerable side.

Stewart said it wasn't dealing with everything from murder and gun crime to road accidents in his job that bothered him, but rather the nagging voices in his head. He described them as 'always there; always chatting to me, and telling me something bad is about to happen'. Invariably, nothing bad ever did *happen.*

Two days prior to one of our weekly phone sessions, he'd been called to a huge incident in the centre of London. However, as he put it: 'The mass brawl involving 30 blokes we helped stop wasn't a big deal, Will; it was the thoughts I had while sitting in the garden yesterday, having a cup of tea.'

Stewart was a keen student who took on all of the Happiness GAP practices. Being the man he was, he did everything I suggested. However, around day 10, he messaged me to say that he was still finding it really hard to put a stop to his anxiety. Meditation wasn't working for him: 'It's just making things worse for me – it's as if the more aware I become of my thoughts, the more worried I become.'

Rather than force Stewart to stick with something that clearly wasn't helping him (even though part of me thought that with enough time, he'd start to get it), I got him onto the idea of doing something that would enable him to be *in the moment, rather than just ticking the box of meditation for the sake of it.*

I asked him if he had a sport or hobby he could start up again, or do more of. He'd played badminton at university, and after some gentle encouragement, he managed to fit back into what he called 'shorts so tight, I'd arrest myself for wearing them!' and head on down to the police centre to see if he could play the odd match there.

After his first game, Stewart called me out of the blue. Our sessions were usually on a Thursday, so at first, I suspected something was up. Instead, I heard him say, 'I'm good, Will; in fact, I haven't felt this good for years. I played like a drunken old man who needs looser shorts, but it didn't matter. It was the release I've been looking for – just good old-fashioned fun.'

It's likely that Stewart's levels of dopamine (a happiness-boosting hormone) had risen due to his being totally immersed in the moment while playing badminton. The mental focus necessary created a 'flow experience' for him. As flow researcher Mihaly Csikszentmihalyi said, 'It's when we act freely, for the sake of the action itself rather than for ulterior motives, that we learn to become more than what we were.'

Stewart was doing nothing more than acting like a kid again – living moment by moment – and yet it was doing his adult body more good than it'd received in years. During a later session he said, 'I now know what they mean when they say I didn't know I had a problem until I started thinking about one. It's as if the less time I spend thinking, the better I feel.'

Stewart wasn't anxious about the huge demands of his job – he was anxious about his thoughts. He didn't 'need' meditation;

he just needed something to do that stopped him thinking for a while. Being in the moment of playing badminton soon helped him realize that his thoughts were just thoughts and, with a higher/wider perspective, he was able to dismiss them more easily.

This boost in Stewart's wellbeing lent extra enthusiasm to his evening gratitude journaling. Whereas before, he'd only come up with a few things, he was now writing 10–20 entries every day on his smartphone. The positive hormonal state that came from his flow experience was likely enabling him to see, feel, hear, smell and taste much more of what was going on around him each day. It was an awesome upward spiral that actually made me feel a little jealous at the time.

Stuart continued coaching for a long while – in each session I'd try to find new and interesting ways to create a flow experience for him and put him into the present moment. Sure, there were frustrating times when he found it difficult to stop his nagging mind – or fit in his badminton (and shorts).

But, over time, Stewart accepted the need to be open-minded about where he got his flow experience, so he could access it without the need for a badminton partner or a functioning hip joint. By the end of our time together, Stewart was an enthusiastic painter, poet and soup-making bread-baker!

The GAP in action

G: Stewart found himself getting into the gratitude journaling as a result of feeling happier from getting back into sport and exercise. *His experience proved that if you do what used to make you happy, the subsequent boost in happiness could make it easier to strengthen your gratitude muscle (creating a positive, upward spiral).*

A: *Stewart had found sport beneficial to his happiness, but like anything cool in life, it normally comes with the duality of its un-cool brother, and in his case this was not being able to do what made him happy all the time. I was so proud of Stewart because through acceptance of this fact he was able to keep his spirits high and have the courage to keep an open mind as to what brought him thought-free joy.*

P: *Stewart really affirmed what it means to be more present; to feel like a kid again; to feel as if you're totally free; and to feel like you haven't a care in the world. Just by playing a sport, Stewart immersed himself in the present moment for long enough each week to gain a wider view of his anxiety.*

Meditation helps many of us because it's immediate and we don't need any special circumstances or equipment to become present. However, what Stewart taught me was that we could do all the meditation in the world, but sometimes, some plain old-fashioned fun and creativity is all we need to get out the way of our overactive minds!

Part II

Filling the Happiness GAP for Life

INTRODUCING LIFELONG GAPINESS

*'The very essence of being human is
that we do not seek perfection.'*

GEORGE ORWELL

Now that you've completed the Happiness GAP programme, we're going to look at ways of filling your Happiness GAP for the rest of your life. This part of the book is about building on the gratitude, acceptance and presence practices and techniques you learned in the 21-day programme to empower, inspire and motivate you to lead the most satisfying, fulfilling, meaningful and pleasurable life possible.

While the 21 days planted 'the seeds of change', the practices I want to take you through now are about showering the growth of your soul with year-round sunlight, water and nutrients (and the occasional G&T).

Shall we?

Pass up 'perfect'

I don't profess to have all the answers for achieving happiness, but I strongly believe that the 'pursuit of perfect' lies at the heart of why many people are in search of things outside themselves for those answers. Perfectionism is something that affects us all – to a greater or lesser degree – in one or more areas at different points in our lives.

Take my client John, for example. He has a very open-minded and nuanced attitude towards parenting, which helps him appreciate the give and take of being a dad, learn how to get better at it, and be compassionate with himself if he messes up from time to time.

However, in contrast with his 'growth-orientated', 'good enough' mindset in that area of his life, John has a very controlling, closed-minded and perfectionist view on how his work life needs to be. This means that when a presentation doesn't go perfectly, he slams himself, causing huge amounts of anxiety and stress.

It also means that John is unwilling to expand his potential in his true passion, as a writer, through fear of change, failure and rejection. John's too scared to take the journey towards his dreams because he doesn't want to be seen as vulnerable and human and 'imperfect'.

Earlier in my life, I had a strong fear of failure born out of wanting to maintain the status quo. My closed-minded view of the world was *I'm just not driven enough to succeed.* This acted as a shield for my true reason for lack of action and growth – fear of 'being seen and getting it wrong'.

Deep down, I didn't want the world to 'see' me, because it would mean *I'd* have to see me, and turning inwards was just plain scary. I wanted to hide from growth because it would be awkward and there was a chance I'd fail or be rejected – a perfectionist's worst nightmare! It's only with hindsight I can fully appreciate why pursuing my dreams has been such a boost to my happiness. Although success has had very little impact on my wellbeing and happiness, the journey towards it *has*.

You see, personal development produces exceptional levels of happiness that can really *only* take place within a mindset of *I'm human, I'll probably get it wrong, but I'm willing to try, fail, learn and grow*. A growth mindset is a mindset that's open to the idea of becoming who we're capable of becoming as creators, parents, lovers, entrepreneurs, friends, contributors to the greater good of society, hobby enthusiasts or anything in between.

As you learned earlier, this growth mindset is what US psychologist Abraham Maslow called 'self-actualization' – where the deepest-held values of the self are aligned with the very same actions. It's what he considered the secret ingredient in those people who were experiencing incredible levels of long-term happiness, energy and motivation. But before we start actualizing your potential by letting go of perfect, I want to dress you up in a Bat suit.

Are you Batman or Superman?

In 2015, the US magazine *Rolling Stone* ran a readers' poll to find the best superhero movie of the modern era. *The Dark Knight* (Batman) was voted number one and *Batman: The Movie* and *The Dark Knight Rises* were both within the top 10.

This isn't just some random trivia you can use in your next pub quiz. I'm telling you this because of who Batman is and why people warm to him. While Spiderman and Superman are 'superhuman', Batman is relatable. He doesn't have 'special' powers that make him perfect and unattainable. He gets hurt, cut and injured easily because he's just a normal bloke (albeit with a ripped body) in an extra-special suit.

> *I want you to be more like Batman – the human that you are – and step away from trying to be Spiderman or Superman.*

I don't think there's anything wrong with aiming for spectacular; it's just that, well, it simply doesn't happen that often. Paradoxically, allowing 'good' to be 'good enough' will unburden you sufficiently to perform more spectacularly as a mum, dad, love-maker, project creator, entrepreneur, gym-goer, joke-teller, chore-doer and life-liver.

When you love yourself enough, value yourself enough, care for yourself enough, you'll notice it's OK to step away from pretending to be invulnerable. Get things wrong and make the odd mistake in your journey towards your potential. In being more like Batman, you can fight the villains and save the day without having to get upset if the Joker gets the better of you every now and then. It's OK to get down, get fed up and get it wrong; I'll explain why in a moment.

The optimism scale

First, I want to show you what positive psychologists call 'the optimism scale'.

1. **Cynicism**: 'Everything is bad and untrustworthy.'

2. **Pessimism**: 'Things are likely to have negative results.'

3. **Realism**: 'Things are the way they are.'

4. **Optimism**: 'Things are likely to have positive results.'

5. **Idealism**: 'Everything will work out brilliantly.'

We can all find ourselves somewhere around all five of these in one day, even in one hour at times. So what is it that sets apart someone who experiences mostly positive emotion from someone who experiences mostly negative emotion? Well, it turns out that what sets happier people apart is not the myriad of daily emotions they experience (for there are plenty of happy people who feel sad even on a daily basis).

As the godfather of positive psychology Martin Seligman pointed out: 'The key difference is the awareness of mind and of thought and subsequent self-created recovery from sad/irrational/worrying thoughts back to the wider view. The ability to recover is the benchmark of a happy person.'

I can relate to Seligman's approach. I'm happier today as an optimist/realist than I was as an idealist/optimist. Years ago, *any* time something went wrong, I'd fall into cynicism. Sure, it was fun riding the wave of positivity on one end, but it hurt for longer periods when life threw me crap. Nowadays, I'm more aware of not needing to fix *all* my problems. I feel as if I allow my problems to be there, alongside me, and have an increased awareness of the need to accept what's outside and inside my control.

Relating the optimism scale to romantic relationships is a neat way of seeing it in action. For example, my wife and I no longer expect each other to be perfect. If I get lazy and forget to take my daughter out to the park to give my wife some downtime during the week, she doesn't slam me for it. She accepts that I might not be perfect, but overall, I'm a good guy.

I don't slam her, either, if she turns me down for sex during the week. Sure, she's my soul mate, but I don't put her on a pedestal, which can only lead to cynicism. We give each other room to be 'good enough' partners and it's left us much happier overall because it's allowed us to grow. We live in a 'good enough' relationship – one that's by no means perfect, but *good enough* to be perfectly happy.

Become more optimistic by filling the GAP

So how does all this relate to the Happiness GAP? Well, my intention with the GAP programme is to put you in the optimal spot for optimism – neither ignoring the crap that needs to be accepted nor focusing too intensely on it. Practising gratitude and being in the present help keep your thoughts above pessimism and negativity, while active acceptance of yourself and others stops you from beating yourself up for trying to be perfect.

The need to acknowledge negative emotion comes from the need to acknowledge a) that it's OK to experience it (thus reducing the subsequent shame/embarrassment that might come from feeling blue/anxious) and b) the idea you can't learn from an experience if you never acknowledged it as real in the first place.

From my extensive research into perfectionism I've found that idealism says *There's nothing wrong with me or my life, and even if there was, there's nothing I could do about it* – an approach that stunts growth and puts things into black-and-white boxes.

Optimism built through cultivating good happiness habits helps create a mindset that says *My life and my psychology could do with some work, which I accept I need to take responsibility for. But, overall, life's pretty darn good.* This approach aims at a happy medium – a nuanced and more open-minded approach to life.

So, let's move on to how you can use gratitude, acceptance and presence to help create lasting happiness in the optimistic sweet spot!

Happiness GAP case study

Will Foster (frustrated, angry, ashamed, and happier)

Throughout my twenties, I suffered greatly from a lack of self-confidence and self-esteem. Then, on a holiday in Sri Lanka, I realized what had been causing me so much pain – being here *(with not great skin caused by psoriasis) and wanting to be* over *there (with great skin). The root cause of my unhappiness wasn't that I didn't have good skin, like the people I envied in the street, but my* thinking *about it.*

Why? Well, you see my thoughts were understandable at the time – red marks on face, elbows, knees and nether regions would piss off even the most spiritual of folk. Annoying thoughts are simply human, but my problems arose because I was taking my thoughts on a stage (or 10!). Here's how:

The GAP in action

G: *It wasn't my skin problem that was hurting me – it was my atrophied gratitude muscle causing a lack of inner strength and resilience to handle it.*

A: *It wasn't my dark thoughts about my skin that were harming me, but my embarrassment, anger and shame in thinking I was 'depressed' or 'freaky' for having them.*

P: *It wasn't my skin problem that was hurting me, but more my wanting to be over* there *while being* here.

When I first started writing my gratitude journal in the evenings and became more openly thankful during the day, I wasn't fussed by the results. After a day spent helping clients, changing nappies and emptying the dishwasher, my back was stiff and tired, and the thought of grabbing my journal was loathsome. What's the point? *I'd think.*

It wasn't until day 14 of the programme that I first tasted something new. I was queuing for a coffee when I felt an ease and enjoyment for being there. It was as if I didn't want to be anywhere else any more.

I wanted to be here – in this queue. I know this sounds minor, but for a guy who'd chased the butterfly of I'll be happy when x happens *for the best part of a decade, it was a big moment. It felt like a shift from 'life will be good when…' to 'life's OK right now – in fact, it's kind of magical.'*

Was it magical in the sense that I'd tapped into a new paradigm a spiritual guru might call higher consciousness? I'd guess so. I'd always been reasonably happy before my skin problem, but my life had never been tested as much as this before.

My ability to handle the psoriasis was low, and although there could be millions of reasons why that was the case, all I knew was that gratitude built me into a stronger version of myself. If the crap that shows up in our lives acts as the fertilizer for growth, my gratitude practice felt like sun and water to that growth.

With hindsight, I can see that much of the blockage in my emotional river wasn't due to psoriasis itself, but to the thought explosions that would take place after I looked at myself in the mirror. Urrghh, my skin looks horrid *was one thing, but I would take those thoughts to the point of* It's so f***ing unfair that everyone else seems to have great skin without even trying. *And* How are clients going to take me seriously when I look like this? *And so on.*

After I took on the 21-day Happiness GAP challenge of accepting anything I couldn't change or alter immediately, a flow returned to my emotional river. Did I still look in the mirror and get down about my skin every now and then? Yes. But it never had the same duration or intensity as before because I was more accepting of what I couldn't change.

If I started to go down 'what can't I control?' rabbit holes of comparing myself to others or how people might perceive me, I simply noticed the thoughts, laughed a little at how silly I was being for trying to battle with something outside my control, and let it go. Simple? Yes. Easy to do? Hell, no!

I wanted to moan, scream and stamp my feet, but what good would it do me? As hard as it was to let go of the struggle I'd created for myself, it was critical I released it because, as I'm sure you'll agree, the story we tell ourselves about who we are and what our life is supposed to be often becomes the reality of what happens in our day to day.

It wasn't just my skin I accepted, either. I changed the negative stories I told myself. How can I be happy if I have to live and work in London instead of by the surf? *became* I can't change where I live or work right now, and that's OK; *and* If only I had more income so I could take my family on holidays and relax a bit more *became* My lifestyle is what it is, and I don't have to get frustrated with that.

I want to make it clear that I'd gone through phases of being more accepting of my life many times before – like after a heady combo of coffee, surfing and sitting in the sun. My good mood dictated whether I was accepting or not. It came and went with the passing conditions of my emotions. If life was good, I let shit go. If it wasn't, I blamed the shit for why I felt like shit.

What difference has the GAP made to my life? Well, it hasn't meant I don't still love caffeine, waves and sun; it's just that I no longer rest my wellbeing on needing the right circumstances for things to be all right. I no longer need life to play fair to feel more satisfied and contented. I can get that from within.

Lifelong Gratitude

'If there was only ever one prayer,
thank you would be enough.'

Meister Eckhart

I love listening to people speak about their departed loved one at a funeral. It's not because I want to be at a funeral, and it's not because I want to see anyone go through emotional heartache, and it's absolutely not because I want to talk with Aunty Sue while eating egg mayonnaise sandwiches at the wake.

It's because I love to hear what people say about the deceased. Most of it is good – no matter how badly he or she treated others. Even if the person was borderline evil, we still try and think of good things to say about them. Don't we?

This is why I'm perplexed that humans spend a lifetime *not saying* what they could say to their circle while they're alive – the kind of things they'd say about them at their funeral: 'John was loved by us all. He was always so giving and offered people his time, energy and enthusiasm. We loved the way he brought a smile to people's faces and how supportive he was to his daughters and wife, no matter how difficult they could be.'

Don't save it for the funeral

What's stopping us from saying things like this to our loved ones today, *now*: in a text message, a card or an email? I don't know exactly. I'm sure I could run a survey asking that question and it would elicit responses like, 'They already know I love them,' or 'They don't need that soppy stuff from me, anyway' or 'It's weird and too deep for me.' The way I see it, the reason most of us hold back is that we're just scared.

When we whittle down our reasons for not saying to someone what we'd say about them at their funeral, it comes down to fear – fear of being 'seen'. Because you see, when we open our heart (and I mean *really* open it, as wide as possible), we're making ourselves vulnerable.

And, according to the wonderful vulnerability researcher Brené Brown, it's *only* in being our most vulnerable that we create a soul-to-soul connection. As she stresses regularly in her book *Daring Greatly*, it's in connecting with other human beings that we fulfil one of our most primal human needs: to feel closely connected with other people.

I've witnessed revolutions of the soul when people write something called 'the funeral letter'. This is a letter/

text message or email that contains all that we'd say about a person at their funeral – except in the *present* tense. It's coming up in the gratitude exercises below.

Adopt an attitude of gratitude

I've long practised this kind of thing; I don't know why. I guess it's because I've always felt the positive effect it has on me and others. I remember when I started doing it, around the age of 16. In a birthday card for the woman who'd been a kind of 'surrogate mum' to me – she'd fed and sheltered me in between my rounds of tennis, football and surfing with my best mate – I expressed how much it meant to me to have that kind of support.

We were in the pub when she opened her card. She cried. We hugged. It was beautiful. And you know, in a world full of angst and stress, wouldn't it be cool to have more of these kinds of moments outside of weddings and funerals?

When we cut away the layers we create for ourselves to prevent the world from seeing who we really are – totally vulnerable and human – we realize we're all in the same boat, and if someone else sees you being totally vulnerable, that gets them right where it gets you: in the heart.

You might be someone who's always been open and honest to the deepest positive emotions you feel towards others. In which case, keep doing what you do! This world needs more you! If you *kind* of do it every now and then, or feel like it could be something you'd like to try, start by reading these words by Brené Brown: 'A deep sense of love and belonging is an irreducible need of all people… When those needs are not met, we don't function as we were meant to….'

I believe the attitude of gratitude goes way beyond an increased ability to see more of the positives in life. It can inspire more feelings of love for everybody involved. It's in giving that we receive, and nowhere could this statement ring more notes of truth than in being openly grateful for what people bring to our lives and why.

Gratitude exercises

I explained earlier how regularly practising gratitude and positivity is like going to a 'happiness gym'. The more you train your mind in a certain way, the easier it is to go back to the same place, over and over. Here are a few more exercises for keeping your gratitude muscle strong for life:

1. Write a 'funeral letter'

Compose a 'funeral letter' to someone at least once a month. The idea is to express *now*, everything you'd say about your loved ones at their funeral. Thank them for all the good they've brought to your life. Opening up your heart in this way is likely to do mysterious and wonderful things for both giver and receiver.

2. Mix it up

Sticking to one way of practising gratitude could lose its novelty over time. So mix things up between writing the gratitude journal and adding gratitude to the end of your daily 10-minute morning meditation. Once the 10 minutes have elapsed, spend a little more time reflecting on what you're grateful for *in that moment*.

Ending your meditation in this way is an awesome way to start the day with extra warmth in your heart, and it keeps the journaling from becoming uninteresting or same old same old. The brain derives so much positive benefit when we keep things new and interesting, and gratitude work is no different.

I recommend going for two to three weeks of journaling on gratitude in the evenings, writing a funeral letter once a month, then switching to just paying attention to what you're grateful for in your morning meditation or mini-med during the day. All this can be mixed up with being openly grateful towards shop assistants, co-workers and people within your close circle.

If you ever notice that your gratitude practice is losing its strength, it's time to switch to other methods. One of my favourites is finding out the name of the person serving me in a supermarket/restaurant/café, etc. I borrowed it from my dad, who used to tell us, 'Get to know people's names – it could transform their day.'

Once you know and use a person's name when thanking them, it increases the power of gratitude for both giver and receiver. Saying 'thank you' to the checkout guy increases the happiness juices, but 'thank you, Dave' can have an even greater effect. Sure, every now and then you might be thought creepy for asking for a name, and be turned down, but do you really care?

3. You attract what you are

If you're not experiencing authentic feelings of gratitude in any given moment, don't feel you 'have' to force it. From what I've seen, some of the 'forcing' of positivity can lead to even more angst (and push happiness and success even further away). As Wayne Dyer put it: 'You do not attract what you want. You attract what you are.'

If you have a rough day, allow yourself to have a rough day and be kinder to your spirit. Being authentic is more important to your mindset (and therefore attraction) than pretending to be positive even when you don't feel it. If you can cultivate authenticity through gratitude and acceptance, you have a recipe for happiness, and therefore success.

4. Notice where your mind is focused

If you start to notice you're finding fault in most situations, it could be that your mind is getting stronger in that direction. Your mind is like a muscle: if you train it in a certain way, it will be strong doing the thing it's being repeatedly taught to do.

For example, if we're constantly judging what people are wearing on the street, moaning about how crappy our job is or wishing we lived in a sunnier climate when it's raining, we're consistently training our minds to be negative.

The more we focus on the negative, the harder it becomes to be positive. If you ever find yourself falling into this cycle, first, don't panic! It's just your mind muscle doing what you've told it to do and it's not your brain's fault! Next, start retraining your gratitude muscle with the gratitude exercises in this book.

The more you're thankful for what's happening in the moment, the easier it is to repeat that the following day, and beyond. This is why your circumstances have very little impact on your happiness – because happiness is dictated by how you *think*.

The more disciplined you are about focusing on what you have, the more you notice how much good there *really is*. It's like refilling the screen wash in your car and restoring a clear view – one that makes it far easier to negotiate the twists and turns of the journey.

I don't want this exercise to confuse you in light of number 3 above; we *all* go through crappier moments. This is just about you, and only you can know who you are and how you manage your mind. Maintain a consistent practice of self-honesty, self-reflection and self-responsibility and you'll never be too far from the good stuff.

5. Don't get burned!

Assessing the state of your love life, finances, body shape or anything in between when you're in a bad mood is like tending to a fire without wearing heat-proof gloves – it's very easy to get burned! If you're in a good mood, you may still have an issue you want to sort out, but the 'glove' of a good mood keeps you from getting burned.

Put simply, when you're in a good mood, is it easier to see the good? The possibilities? The reasons to be hopeful? And is the reverse true when you're in a bad mood? Is it harder to see the cool stuff, get things done or feel hopeful?

With this in mind, beware assessing the state of your life when you're tired or run-down. Not only will you get very little done, you'll likely create a 'negative bias', leaving you feeling even worse about the situation you're trying to sort.

This insight played out while I was writing this book. Before I grew in self-awareness, I would read through my writing at the end of a hard week, when I was worn out. In doing this, I created all kinds of negative spirals born out of clouded judgement and tiredness. The following morning, after some solid rest, I'd read through the *exact* same work and feel optimistic and pleased by it.

I'm not suggesting you become overly optimistic and cloud your judgement too much towards the positive.

This is about acknowledging that you can only judge things clearly if your head is in a clear state.

If you're knackered and run-down, you'll probably get burned trying to sort out your life without your heat-proof gloves! Instead, have self-awareness of your state, be disciplined about leaving things alone, get some rest, come back clearer the next day and even if there is a fire to tend to, at least you'll be protected from getting burned!

Enough now means more tomorrow

If you're looking to make more money, sculpt the body of your dreams, meet a loving partner, do a job you love, heal a difficult relationship – anything – the power of gratitude to create the life of your dreams is immense. When you're in a grateful place, you're coming from a vibration that tells the Universe *I have enough*.

In this place of contentment, you're vastly more empowered to achieve your goals – the more your creative, productive and inspired faculties come to life, the happier you'll be, and you'll be coming from strong desire (a very powerful attractor) and not discontented neediness.

When you come from a place of need, it tells the Universe you don't have enough already (which serves to push away what you're looking to attract). When you come from a gentler, calmer and overall happier energy of 'want' and desire, the things you're looking to attract will turn up in all kinds of coincidental ways.

And at the heart of this energy shift is gratitude. Whereas an ungrateful ego tells the Universe *I don't have enough yet*, a grateful heart tells it *I have all that I need already – everything on top is what I 'want'*.

On hundreds of occasions, I've witnessed the power of gratitude to attract more into people's lives. Once you've trained your gratitude muscle sufficiently, don't be surprised when all kinds of mysterious and wonderful things start to show up from almost nowhere!

Be thankful for life's crap

> *'The crap that shows in life acts like the fertilizer to personal growth and development.'*
> PATTI RENNER

A good way to see the potential benefit to your downturns, annoyances and hurtful moments is to view the people and situations you've found most difficult as your 'teachers'. Through the 'what is she/he teaching me?' lens, people and situations no longer have the disempowering effect they might once have had.

Nelson Mandela taught us the power in this lesson in his life. In his book *The Long Walk to Freedom*, he said, 'As I walked out the door toward the gate that would lead to my freedom, I knew if I didn't leave my bitterness and hatred behind, I'd still be in prison.'

Personally, I'm thankful for my psoriasis. It has given me my purpose, my struggle, my story, and without it, my life wouldn't have become as rich, deep or meaningful. It has given me more than I could ever have hoped for in life: the chance to help others avoid the pitfalls of 'destination seeking' that I'd made for so many years.

If this book helps a single person avoid sacrificing present happiness for future destinations, I'll die a happy man. My psoriasis taught me it's OK to suffer and that it's important to acknowledge and accept it fully. It makes us stronger, wiser and more appreciative of the good times. A life without suffering or pain is a life unlearned and unlived.

All you need to know about the story of your life is that it had to happen the way it did to make you who you are today. You might not be able to eliminate all the problems and stressors that cross your path, but you can choose to take the lessons from them.

Gratitude exercise

You can use the technique of reframing – putting a positive spin on 'negative' events – to take the crap thrown on your path as 'fertilizer' for your personal growth. Here are some examples from which you can create your own 'reframes'.

Event: Client doesn't show up for a therapy session.

Reaction: Worrying thoughts about how to pay the bills with an unreliable income.

Fertilizer: What can I do now to make the best of this situation? What can I do so I'm thankful for this situation that I can't control?

Growth: Sit in a coffee shop and enjoy an hour's reading for pleasure; and the resulting growth in your ability to remain calm throughout the rough-and-tumble of life.

Event: Someone says something hurtful to you.

Reaction: Feelings of pain, anger and resentment.

Fertilizer: What is this person teaching me about how I want to feel? What am I thankful for in this person?

Growth: I'm thankful I'm not in their skin! I can only imagine how much pain they must be in to say what they've said. Thank the heavens I'm me!

Event: A first date goes badly.

Reaction: Thoughts like *Never again* and *There are no good ones out there any more.*

Fertilizer: What have I got to be thankful for right now? Do I now know, with deeper clarity, what I *don't* want in a partner?

Growth: Stronger conviction to keep looking for the person I do want instead.

Event: Lack of money, time or energy prevents the pursuit of a dream.

Reaction: Thoughts of dread at having to continue living current lifestyle.

Fertilizer: I know I don't have much money right now, but what other forms of wealth do I possess – in my health or relationships?

Growth: Feelings of gratitude, and subsequent resilience to life's crap, leading to a more productive mindset regarding finances.

Event: A health condition rears its ugly head.

Reaction: Thoughts and feelings of anger, resentment and bitterness.

Fertilizer: What is this condition teaching me about how better to manage my body and my stress levels?

Growth: Feelings of empowerment and self-responsibility around the kind of human you want to choose to be – now and in the future.

Have a moment of introspection

If you want to go a stage further and add some happiness rocket fuel to life's crap, ask yourself if there's a meaning to it all. Reflecting on your life, where it's heading and why, could be vital to your happiness. In today's society people often know more about the lives of the family down the road, politicians and celebrities than they do their own.

This is because introspection can be scary. It's a rare human being who can look inwards and ask *Why did I do that? What's the meaning behind it all and how can I grow as a result of it?* rather than pointing the finger at everything or everyone else.

The funny thing about fear is how illusionary it is. Having a moment of introspection might seem scary, but once it's done, all the concerns about getting to know who you really are fly out the window. And once you appreciate that growth is waiting on the other side of fear, you'll appreciate how many dreams you still have.

Dreams you were born with; dreams you are attached to, like a perfectly woven seam in the garment of your being; dreams that you can allow to come to the surface, or dreams that will stay within you until you reach your deathbed. Don't let it be the latter. Take the meaning behind it all, seek the learning, and never let fear get in the way of you journeying towards the growth of your dreams!

Gratitude exercise

Sit for a few moments right now and reflect on a life lesson you've been through. Ask yourself how it could lead to the next chapter in your life. In your journal, write down one to five deep questions about the lesson.

I'm adamant that clients set goals for a number of reasons, but the main one is self-discovery. It's not the work that you'll love journeying towards your summit, but who you discover yourself to be along the way. Here are some examples of how your 'self-questioning' could look:

- Did that failed relationship hurt and suck and teach me what it means to be with a partner – the taste of incredible happiness that comes from being in love? Do I have the courage and self-honesty to keep that in mind as motivational juice for my next step?

- Did that failed attempt at starting a business hurt and suck and teach me how much richer and more fulfilling life was feeling as I moved towards a goal with a greater sense of purpose? What do I want my goal for? To have the victory or to live a richer and more meaningful life that doesn't back down from challenge?

- Did that health problem scare the crap out of me and teach me the importance of good health? Of what it really means to live in 'true wealth'? Could I keep this knowledge close to me and help inspire others about what true wealth means?

We can either become apathetic about our past failings or use gratitude to see the purpose behind it all. It's in finding the deeper meaning to your life's setbacks that you'll find inspiration to move your life to a new dawn.

Crap can suck. And it will. Just don't let it pass you by without asking, 'What do I want this event to mean to my life as I move forward?' As holocaust survivor Viktor Frankl declared, 'Man does not simply exist but always decides what his existence will be, what he will become in the next moment. By the same token, every human being has the freedom to change at any instant.'

Lifelong Gratitude recap

▶ Who would you like to improve your rapport with over the next 10, 20 or even 40 years? Could you send them the 'funeral letter' containing positive things you'd say about them at their funeral? Don't leave anything unsaid.

▶ Mix up your gratitude practice between journaling, writing letters and being openly grateful to people face to face. Could you reframe some of the crap that shows up in your life in the light of some of the nuggets of wisdom you've learned while doing the GAP programme?

LIFELONG ACCEPTANCE

*'Whatever you resist persists and
whatever you fight you strengthen.'*

Eckhart Tolle

As you experienced on days 16–21 of your GAP programme, acceptance is most effective at creating flow in our emotional river if we approach it from two levels.

The two levels of lifelong acceptance

To recap, level 1 acceptance is where we allow real emotions to be acknowledged as real and 'there'. In the long term, the aim of level 1 acceptance is to continue your own path of self-discovery.

Maybe the GAP programme brought up emotions you'd suppressed? Maybe it didn't – and if so, don't go worrying about it, thinking there might be something wrong with you in this regard. If you've always allowed yourself to feel what you feel (and don't suppress it), you probably have a very free-flowing emotional river.

Either way, level 1 acceptance is about letting go of the idea we could ever be perfect humans, putting down our shields and seeking to understand what feelings are inside us and why.

At level 2 acceptance, we ask ourselves, 'What could I accept as being within my control?' Sure, many of the things we experience in life are beyond our control – for example, the way people can be, the weather, our current life circumstances. In the coming section, we're going to take a look at how you can continue to keep your emotional river unblocked, smooth and free-flowing – for the rest of your life.

Here's a summary of the two levels of lifelong acceptance:

- **Level 1: Accepting the reality of now – of 'what is'.** The question becomes: 'Does the person who never accepts their authentic range of human emotions ever feel true happiness?'

- **Level 2: Accepting that we all have the potential for future change – of what is yet to be.** The question becomes: 'Does the person hiding behind the curtain of pretending everything's OK (when it's not) ever give themselves a chance to grow into the person they're capable of becoming?'

Accepting 'what is' takes a conscious awareness of the present moment – of how we're thinking, feeling and behaving around a situation. Like in the Serenity Prayer, which urges us to accept what we can't change and have the courage to change what we can, we must ask ourselves two more questions: 'Is this something that's *outside* my control, and must I therefore accept it for what it is?' And 'Is this something that, with enough courage, vision and action, I can actually *change*?'

Accepting 'what is' helps you live a happier life, while accepting that we all have the potential for future change assists you in living a happier, inspired life. Let's take a more in-depth look at level 1 acceptance first:

Level 1: Accepting 'what is'

'The parkland oak tree just is.

It doesn't judge or try and change anything.

It stands in the wind, rain, sun and snow without a fuss.

It saw German fighter planes drop bombs on the nearby town in the summer of 1944, and school fetes in the same town the following year.

It has witnessed ugly fights, passionate lovemaking, over-50s football matches, teenagers playing Pokemon on their smartphones and everything in between.

How does the oak tree relate to you?

It's part of nature – and so are you.'

In this moment we share together, ask yourself: 'Do I accept my self for who I am and my life for what it is?' True happiness isn't just about feeling more joy and pleasure. It's like the man or woman who puts up a shield of strength to stop anyone hurting them in future relationships: the shield may protect them from the darkness of heartache and rejection, but it also serves to block out the potential for joy and love.

In rejecting our true emotions, we deny the chance for real happiness – the kind that takes place only when we make ourselves vulnerable to heartache, failure and setbacks.

To deny your true nature – the reality of your vulnerability and emotions – is to deny that we live in a world of duality: happy/sad, positive/negative, light/dark. Our nature is something we're blessed and cursed with at the same time, and if we can't accept that our flaws, fears and weaknesses are 'OK' and part of being human, how can we ever learn from them and become wiser?

As Brené Brown says in *Daring Greatly*, when we 'close our spiritual doors to the darkness it stops us from learning what we need to know to allow more light to enter'.

Accepting the reality of your true feelings

Now I'm going to take you through the two ways in which acceptance of 'what is' works for the things you *cannot* change right away – those outside your control.

I once watched an interview with American big-wave surfer Greg Long that provides a neat example of accepting the true reality of our emotions as a vital mechanism for happiness and growth.

Long had just won a big-wave event, but said that competing in it had been an ego-driven mistake. Just three weeks earlier, he'd had a near-death experience while surfing, almost drowning before being brought back to life.

Long described how he'd lied to himself before the competition, pretending to be OK about being back out in the ocean so soon after his experience. He later faced up to his truth – the reality of post-traumatic stress – found help among his peers and other professionals and is now competing with the same vigour he was before.

I truly believe the greatest human strength is the ability to be weak; to admit our vulnerabilities and drop the guard of 'I need to be strong and tough so I don't get hurt or seem weak.' You need to let go of what the world might think about you going through a real human moment.

Rejecting true emotion, through shame, embarrassment or anger, dams our emotional flow. Acceptance breaks the dam and restores it. I love how speaker and coach Robert Holden says that 'a feeling has only one ambition in life and that is to be felt. You can't be truly happy and untruthful of your sadness.'

Take action on Holden's wise words and allow yourself permission to feel each emotion to its fullest. All pain arrives and leaves, but it's when you put up a block to pain that it hangs around and lingers and creates blockages in your emotional river.

Accepting your life

In the past, one of the things I found hardest to accept about my life was living in London, away from my beloved Devon coastline. For almost a decade, a wave of depression hit me each time I drove back from the beach to the Big Smoke. London's mix of stressed-out people, long commutes and lack of coast/countryside was hard to accept. My thought process was, 'How on earth did I end up here? This is brutal!'

My discontent continued for a few more years, until one Thursday evening after a busy train journey home from work. As I walked down the station platform and into our local park, a beautiful sunset shot orange rays like arrows through the oak trees in the distance. And I realized something: I was doing this to myself! Just as had happened in Sri Lanka, it dawned on me how much of my unhappiness was being generated not by outside circumstances, but by how I was *choosing to think*.

You've got to love yourself and be brave enough to let go. To let go and allow your life to be what it is now and not how you thought it should've turned out. Waiting to be happy once you have everything you want is like waiting for a bus that may never come. Choosing to be happier now gets you on the bus this moment – right here.

And the coolest part about the whole thing? It's only ever one brave and bold thought away. I've witnessed this on hundreds of occasions working one to one with clients. The moment we stop fighting with the reality of our life, the angst we so often hide from the outside world about living a life we don't like can no longer arise in the same way.

If you're willing to accept your finances, career, love life, health, relationships, lifestyle or anything in between as it is *now*, you'll have a spirit waiting to give you the warmest hug you may ever have felt.

Level 2: Accepting the potential for future change

'We may place blame, give reasons, and even have excuses, but in the end, it's an act of cowardice not to follow our dreams.'

Dr Steve Maraboli, behavioural scientist

Next, we're going to take a look at the second part of lifelong acceptance and see what you can change. Accepting 'what is' doesn't mean giving up on rewriting your future. In fact, it's what helps you write the first words of your next chapter.

Why cut coconuts?

If you and your loved ones were to live on a desert island for the rest of your lives, what do you think would make you feel discontented there? The absence of mirrors, TVs, social media, modern gadgets, shopping centres or shiny cars, or the knowledge that anyone else existed?

If all you ever needed was already with you, what would be left for you to feel down about? Would it be that you didn't feel pretty enough in your grass skirt? Would it be that you didn't feel successful as a coconut-cutter? Would it be that you hadn't built the tree house in the right part of the jungle?

In the end, would the reason behind your wanting to become a successful coconut-cutter be a desire to beat all the other cutters on the island? Or would you just love cutting coconuts as part of the creative being that you are? As George Orwell said, 'happiness can only exist in acceptance', and a huge part of that deal is accepting the potential for change and becoming the coconut-cutter you know you *can* become.

The answer is twofold. Firstly, cutting coconuts is flow-based. As you learned during the 21-day GAP programme, when someone is immersed in a challenging activity – 'in the flow' – it switches on the ingenious/instinctive part of the brain and turns off the analytical part (the one that conjures worrying thoughts out of thin air!).

As the ancient Greek philosopher Plato pointed out, 'The greatest wealth is to live content with little.' I can't think of a better way to live in that space than to be immersed passionately in something you're working towards. The longer we spend being free from intellectual thought, the longer we get to spend being free from over-thinking our day-to-day worries.

This is one of the primary reasons I wanted you to experience flow (or at least plant the seeds of flow) during the GAP programme, and it's why I want you to accept room for creating the future of your dreams. The second reason to become the coconut-cutter you can become is what is says to your inner psyche.

As Carl Rogers, one of the founders of the humanistic approach towards psychology, pointed out in his research, the path to becoming a highly functioning person requires developing increasing trust in your ability to know what's important to you; what is essential for you to live a more fulfilling life.

Rogers believed that optimal humans listen to that nagging feeling inside that they're not becoming who they can be, and accept self-responsibility. Remember how I likened acceptance to a free-flowing river? Well, much of the blockage we create inside that river comes from denying the reality of our true emotions and how life 'is'; it also stems from a lack of action towards achieving our deeply held goals and dreams.

Will you keep pretending, or decide to go?

I have a passionate belief that we mustn't pretend we don't *want* to become who we can become, because the more we lock away our dreams, the more we lock away the potential for happiness through a sense of growth that comes from being on the inspired path (more on this later).

If you just want to be happier, it's time to accept your true emotions and the way things are in your life. To fight with the reality of what you don't like about yourself or your life is like getting annoyed with gravity when a tennis ball comes back to Earth after being thrown into the air. *It just is. It's there.* It's real, and there's no need to try controlling something that's outside your control – at least for now.

Once you've declared to the Universe what you can't change in this moment, is there a part of you that dreams of travelling on an inspired path towards becoming the person you're capable of becoming? In my experience as a coach, the biggest reason people don't follow their dreams is not because they don't have any, but because they're afraid to take action in case they get hurt.

But, you see, there's a way you can avoid becoming worried about getting hurt. How? By moving onto the 'good enough' path.

Perfectionism vs 'good enough'

Imagine there are two paths through life: the first is the icy slope of perfectionism and the second is the soft grassy path of 'good enough'.

When a perfectionist climbs towards his dreams, the slightest trip impacts more than it should because it's slippery underfoot and he slides down into cynicism. For example, if he tries online dating and is rejected for a second date, his slide into cynicism has him saying, 'There are no good women out there – they're all awful.' Or if he starts a T-shirt business that absorbs more money than it makes in its first year, he thinks: *This is no good, there's obviously no money in T-shirts!*

Perfectionists tend to jump onto images of black and white: *she's an idiot; he's a loser; that idea was rubbish; this project's never going to happen.* Perfectionists get crappy results on the inspired path (as we all do from time to time!), but they decide to give up sooner by putting failure inside a box marked 'tried that, didn't work, not trying again'.

Why? Well, it's mainly because perfectionists don't ever like to assume that *they* are the ones causing the failures. They tend to blame outside circumstances to keep themselves safe from potential pain and suffering.

This is simply human in many ways, but in denying the reality of how bumpy the inspired path is going to be, we deny ourselves the spiritual gold dust contained in picking ourselves back up after a failure and telling the Universe: 'I now know why that happened – and next time, I'm going to do things this way.'

What we tell ourselves on the inspired path does more for our personal growth and happiness than reaching the destination itself. It's the people we have to become to have success that creates huge leaps in happiness.

Perfectionists leap at the idea of things either working or not working. But the truth is, we need to accept that anything worth having in life takes time, effort and an incredible amount of perseverance. As Andy Dufresne remarked after crawling through 3km of poo pipes to escape from prison in the movie *The Shawshank*

Redemption: 'Hope is a good thing, maybe the best of things, and no good thing ever dies'.

Walking the path of 'good enough'

On the flip side, when we accept there's not a straight line to success and happiness, it's like moving off the icy slope and onto a soft grassy path. It's that lovely fresh-cut grass here, and for extra lush-ness, I want you to visualize that you've kicked off your shoes! The ice has melted, which makes it softer and easier underfoot. When we trip on the grassy path of good enough, we still get hurt and, of course, it still sucks. After all, who wants life to take an unplanned turn?

But while the perfectionist would've slid 50 metres down the icy slope into cynicism and blaming outside factors, to keep emotional discomfort at arm's length, those on the 'good enough' path fall where they fall. They don't go anywhere, and after some time to acknowledge healing and hindsight, they start making steps forward again. It's this single factor – staying in the game for long enough – that overall is the secret to success (and happiness).

It's about never giving up. It's about always learning. Always moving forward. Always staying optimistic. No matter how slow it can feel sometimes. No matter how badly you may have failed, been rejected or got it wrong, each fall contains nuggets of wisdom you can take with you on the next stage in your journey towards the summit. Nuggets you would never have known before –

how to avoid those kinds of potholes, how to move past those kinds of rocks, or how to get round those kinds of waterways.

How would you know how to navigate obstacles on the path if you'd never learned from previous mistakes? Your path to greater levels of success and happiness will never be a perfect one. The moment you expect it to be is the same moment the obstacles will have a greater impact on your progress than they should.

Moving with the goal

My wife recently gave me a fantastic insight into the 'good enough' path. On our way back from a workout, I asked her how she'd found it. 'It was OK,' she said. 'Initially I got a bit frustrated because I didn't have as much energy as I thought I did. I had this idea of doing 10 rounds of sprints, but after the first round, I figured five or six would be better than nothing.'

Without even being aware she was doing it, her acceptance of a 'good enough' workout (and not a perfect one) had an 'allowing-ness' to it that enabled her to 'move with the goal'. A good enough workout would be good enough, and it meant she still felt she'd accomplished something positive by the end.

On the flip side, I recall a personal-training client who never felt she'd done enough in the day. She'd set these crazily high expectations for what she wanted to achieve in a week and almost always fall short. She wasn't even aware that she'd been operating with this mindset until she experimented with a different approach.

In hindsight, she was able to see how sick, worried and depressed her perfectionism used to make her. Near the end of our time together, she came into sessions a bit more relaxed and ready to do what her body would allow on the day. Roughly eight times out of 10, her performance improved. Her 'allowing-ness' for accepting the inevitable twists and turns led to greater overall success and higher self-esteem.

'Good enough' is more fun, too!

In his book *In The Pursuit of Perfect*, Tal Ben-Shahar calls this willingness to move with the goal posts 'Optimalism' – the ability to remain optimistic throughout the inevitable twists and turns on the inspired journey.

Shahar defines perfectionists as 'rigid, static, only one way to get to where he or she wants to go...feelings are irrelevant to decision-making process; obsessive need for control, change is the enemy, improvisation too risky, playfulness unacceptable'. 'Optimalists', meanwhile, are 'adaptable, dynamic, also sets ambitious goals for his or her self but is not chained to these commitments; does not charter direction according to a rigid map'.

I can testify to the 'playfulness unacceptable' part of perfectionism. When I first started making online videos,

I wrote scripts, orchestrated lighting and tried my hardest to remember my lines and make perfect videos. The results were dismal. I sounded like an idiot and they never captured the real me.

I just didn't have the set-up or experience to create what I thought was good enough content. Not only that, I was stressed and not having much fun either. When I hadn't produced a perfect video, I slid down the icy slope into 'Screw this online stuff – it's all a load of crap!'

Midway through my online journey, I read Shahar's book and when I implemented his philosophy I got much better results. I ditched the scripts, lighting and trying to remember lines and went back to just being myself and making videos that were good enough to be good enough. As a result, not only was I less stressed, I was happier and having more fun too. The words flowed more naturally, my personality shone through and people warmed to the authenticity of what I was creating.

As a perfectionist I felt like a producer of content; as an 'Optimalist' walking on the grassy path of good enough, I felt like a creator. It helped me achieve more in six months than I'd done in the previous three years! Planning your strategy gets you moving forward. Just remember not to get too hooked up on it. As the 34th president of the USA Dwight D. Eisenhower once said, 'In preparing for battle I have always found that plans are useless, but planning indispensable.'

Success = happiness vs happiness = success

If you can accept that you have the potential for change in an area of your life in which you'd love to move forward, I want to ask you a question about your path towards a more inspired life.

Imagine you have a genie who will grant you everything you want – the perfect family, perfect partner, perfect house, perfect body, perfect career, perfect friends, perfect bank balance, perfect amount of time for holidays – everything.

But there's a catch: you can have all this cool stuff, but you cannot also have inner peace and contentment. Would you still take it? If your answer is, 'Yes, I'd still like this incredibly appealing list of great things, and I'll skip the inner peace. Thanks for the offer though, Will', it doesn't make you a bad person. It just means that because you've been living in the Western paradigm of success = happiness for so long, your wiring towards spiritual freedom is a little frayed.

Teachers telling us that we need to get good grades if we want to be happy and successful; sculpted bodies on the covers of magazines and straplines shouting 'Lose weight and get back the happiest you'; or Instagram gurus saying, 'Look at me living by the ocean as I sip green juices in between hugs from my husband, dog, children and massive following' haven't helped this paradigm much either.

Social media has warped our sense of what *is* real as opposed to what just *seems* real. I still get caught up in the success = happiness paradigm in moments of weakness. But you know, if the success = happiness paradigm were true, wouldn't every person who got what they wanted be incredibly happy? I'm sure we all know people who have lots of stuff but are still constantly chasing the destination. It doesn't matter how much someone has on the outside, if they don't feel good on the inside, they can't enjoy it.

What would you take?

So, would you opt for contentment over all the 'perfect' stuff? If so, the irony is that in accepting how things are now, the pressure to 'succeed' is reduced, which empowers all of your potential to succeed. And in the most important way possible – *your* way! The way that matters to you and your values (instead of those of well-meaning parents, peers and society).

Happiness = success because the happier you are, the more creative, inspired, motivated, and most importantly, accepting you are of the imperfect and 'good enough' path towards success. Whatever your path delivers to you, it's essential that from time to time you allow yourself 'permission to wanna pack it all in' or PTWPIAN.

A case of the PTWPIANs is a normal human syndrome, but one that, I believe, only lasts when we're walking the icy slope of perfectionism. You have an inner coconut-cutter who wants you to succeed and grow in all areas of your life. Not because it wants success for you (although that's always nice). It wants to get you inspired about cutting coconuts. Period.

Bringing this 'growth' mindset together becomes a pretty funky hiking party when you boil it down to this question: 'Are you going to cut coconuts on a grassy path dressed in a Bat suit? Or not?'

Lifelong Acceptance recap

▶ What can you accept as being *outside* your control? Can you live alongside the natural order of your thoughts, feelings and life, as nature does?

▶ What can you accept as being *inside* your control? Is there a Bat-suited coconut-cutter inside you who could walk on the sunnier side of life?

Happiness GAP case study

Lisa (grumpy on a Monday, and happier)

In the middle of one coaching session, Lisa – a client who'd been struggling to find the right work/life balance – suddenly said, 'Oh Will, I'm so annoyed with myself for drinking so much over the weekend. I feel terrible. I've lost my temper at work twice already today, and I feel a mess. Why do I do this to myself?'

'It's OK, Lisa, we all mess up from time to time.' I replied. 'But can I ask – did you have a good time with your pals?'

'Well, yeah, I had a blast,' Lisa said.

'In that case, you don't have to feel bad for having a fun time. Sure, you don't feel wonderful right now, but that's to be expected. You know the GAP programme you went through before your last holiday? Overall, were you happier during that time than when you were out and about doing the usual social/drinking thing? This is purely observational; I'm just interested to know.'

'It's hard to know from here because I feel pretty crappy,' Lisa replied. 'But when I stop to think about it, I probably was a little happier when I'd accepted I had the power to change and wasn't drinking.'

'Well, it's seems to me there's one Lisa with the identity of a partygoer – the life and soul of any social event – and another Lisa who's quite happy leading a simple, healthy and happy life. Is that a fair observation?' I went on.

'Well, yeah, I guess so. I do genuinely have a passion and love for being social and going out a lot, though. But I know I can't have that lifestyle and feel wonderful come Monday,' Lisa admitted.

'Something you've just said is so profound, Lisa.' I remarked. 'Consciously or not, you said: "I know I can't have that lifestyle and feel..." You are trying to "have it all". You want to feel incredible and go out drinking – but the two simply don't go hand in hand.

'Somewhere along the line, it might be a cool idea to focus on what you have already, in the form of a great social life. Accept your good vitality as good enough, try being with the moment come Monday, and move away from regretting something you did in the past that you cannot change.

'If a good enough level of vitality is not OK for you right now, let's make a change; if it is OK, then just accept good as being good enough. This is simply about knowing yourself well enough to know where you want to sit.'

Lisa continued her practice of drinking heavily on the weekend, but with a twist – she was much happier doing so. Despite the occasional slip into old habits, she's happier for accepting her Monday moods. For some of us, acceptance acts as the catalyst for change – the kind that turns life into an inspired journey. For others, acceptance simply brings back the peace and flow that we're all looking for.

Has Lisa stopped drinking? No. Is she happier living her current life? Yes. As she said in one of our sessions a while back: 'You don't have to change your life, to change your life.'

The GAP in action

G: *Lisa felt happier when she paid more mental attention to the cool stuff in her life, such as the great friendship circle she got to hang out with on weekends.*

A: *She learned to accept that being in a yucky mood on a Monday came with the duality inherent in having a fun time drinking on the weekend as part of her chosen lifestyle. Her self-acceptance affirmation was 'Come rain or shine, I'm gonna accept my life of work and wine.'*

P: *She was no longer caught in the 'no-man's-land' of regretting having got drunk come Monday morning, or wishing she was at the pub on a healthy night in with her partner come Friday night. She simply practised being more in the moment of her yucky Monday and didn't wish she could change the present.*

LIFELONG LIVING IN THE PRESENT

'Wherever you go – there you are.'

JON KABAT-ZINN, FOUNDER OF THE MINDFULNESS-BASED
STRESS REDUCTION (MBSR) PROGRAMME

One of the primary reasons humans aren't as optimistic as they could be is their belief in the illusory idea that the past and future are *real* places. They give power, energy and reason to the past as a justification for their feelings in the present. Likewise, they see their current situation as a means to justify worrying about what the future will bring.

In this chapter we'll be looking at how you can tune in to your mind to continue the presence work you began during the 21-day GAP programme.

Tuning in to your deeper self

I want to make it clear that the Happiness GAP programme does not offer a cure for clinical anxiety or depression, or past trauma. That said, becoming more present with life *can* leave folk who tend to let thoughts of future destinations or past mistakes take over the joy of the present moment, a whole lot happier. How? Well, when we're aware of the 'now', we naturally become more mindful of which thoughts help our happiness and which ones hinder it.

Imagine working in a room with an ugly painting on the left wall and a lovely outside view on the right. Where do you focus your attention? Are you offended by the ugly painting? Do you question who on earth would buy something like that, and get annoyed that you're going to have to stare at it for the remainder of your day? Or do you notice the painting, shrug your shoulders and then turn your attention to how uplifting it is to have a beautiful view to your right?

Are you present with your thinking in the moment-to-moment of your day? Are you aware of how it makes you feel? Mind expert Michael Neill says that 'We believe our minds are like cameras, taking pictures of exactly what's going on around us, but in fact, they're more like projectors – taking in images and projecting them into our minds from there.'

If, therefore, a person thinks the past hurt them so much that they can't be happy in the present, they're right. That is their reality because that's how they choose to focus their attention. If someone thinks the future is bleak (especially after reading and watching the news every day), and that's the reason they can't (or shouldn't) feel good now, they're right too. It's one gigantic, cosmic, universal, self-fulfilling prophecy.

The adaptation effect

Beyond the roof over your head and the food in your belly, all that you want or want rid of is an illusion. You will adapt. You will get used to your new surroundings. If you're forever seeking the future as your place of salvation, you'll forever be unhappy. As you learned in the introduction, this 'adaptation effect' means that no matter what new job, partner, success or lifestyle you come into, life will resume being normal after the high has worn off.

Improving your circumstances can't give you what you're looking for, until you've tuned in to your mind – because how you feel is created by how you think. If someone is a 'glass half empty' kind of guy or gal (i.e. a pessimist), no improvement in personal circumstances can change what can only be changed from within. As the ancient Greek philosopher Socrates pointed out, 'He who is not contented with what he has, would not be contented with what he'd like to have.'

Living a happier life isn't about eliminating all of life's crap. It's about working out how you can operate in a happier mindset despite it.

Isn't that what we're missing in this life? Because there will always be something to complain about with the glass-half-empty mindset. Even if the glass-half-empty person does get rid of x or accumulate y, they're still operating in the same mindset, so there will just be something new to moan and complain about.

I guess it comes back to a choice we make in the present moment: either wait for life to play fair before we feel good (which, at least in my experience, can be a very LONG wait!) or choose to feel good anyway and declare that you are the master of your own ship, deciding where *you* want it to sail.

Your search for peace ends when you realize it's resting here, in this moment. That's where the good stuff lies. So, how do you achieve more of the good stuff for today and the rest of your life? By training your mind to notice more of it, and that's what we're going to look at next.

The Universal Mind

'Mindfulness is defined as "maintaining a moment-by-moment awareness of our thoughts, feelings, bodily sensations, and surrounding environment."'

JON KABAT-ZINN

Throughout my life, my loss of mental health has rarely come from a lack of wanting to think positively, but more from trying to force it back. For example, in the face of negative thoughts, I used to think, *I don't want this thought or feeling. Go away, go away…think more positive thoughts.*

This just made things worse. Why? Because the more we try to rid ourselves of negative thoughts, the more strength we give to them. Once we're in a neurotic battle with our own thinking, force is met with more force and the spiral goes on. Can you empathize with this?

Sometimes, I'll be wandering home after a pleasant day coaching clients when, out of nowhere, my thoughts start running along these lines: *What's this? Something bad? I'm supposed to be a positive guy, and positive people don't have shitty thoughts. Why can't I get over this?* Without what's known as a 'Universal Mind' connection and awareness, I can become totally lost in my own thoughts.

So what is the Universal Mind? It's the infinitely peaceful bit of you that's aware you're having a thought. For instance, when you sit here now, who's reading these words? I know it's you, but *who is the bit that's aware it's you who is aware it's you*? That deeper level of awareness is the only place you'll find peace because it's the dwelling in which non-judgement resides.

It's the bit of you that only observes thoughts, people, events and stressors for what they are, from a place of non-judgement. Before learning about mindfulness meditation, I thought I was crazy, having the kinds of thoughts I had. The line between sanity and insanity is so fine, yet the feelings could not be more different.

A tremendous amount of self-trust and courage is built when we can go from *Get rid of the bad thought now…go back to happy, go back to happy* to *I'm having this crappy thought and it too shall pass.* It's about reminding ourselves that the more we don't want to be in *this* moment, the longer the pain will last.

When we bring the physical body to eliminating bad thoughts, the more physical pain we go through. When, on the other hand, we bring spiritual presence to a bad thought, it dissipates almost immediately. When you raise your awareness and connect with the Universal Mind, it's as if you can see thoughts playing in your head, like a movie.

Unlock a deeper awareness of NOW!

Once you can separate your spiritual self from your physical self, you'll be able to stay calm and collected, no matter what your brain wants to produce in that moment. Here are two analogies that illustrate what I mean about having a deeper awareness of the present; they also reveal how you can avoid getting worried about worrying thoughts.

The cinema

Imagine that deeper awareness of the present is a cinema. Your awareness/Universal Mind inside your soul is the person sitting in the auditorium and the thoughts coming in and out of your mind are like the movie being played on the screen.

Sometimes the movie will be scary, and at other times it will be joyous. The key is knowing that *you* are not part of the movie – it's just a movie. Thoughts are just thoughts and you don't have to control every single one you have.

You *can choose* to let the movie play without having to jump inside the screen and change the picture!

Fred the cat

Imagine that a thought you don't like or want is a stray cat called Fred. (He/she can be a Keith the Dog or Albert the Rabbit or John the Bear if you don't want to use a cat. The only thing with it being John the Bear is the need for a bear flap on your front door…bet they have them in Canada…if they don't, the world needs bear flaps for bears…but then loads of bears would find themselves in people's living rooms in Canada…I'll shush now).

Now, you're just relaxing on the sofa chilling out when Fred (or Keith or Albert) enters through the cat flap into the living room of your mind. At this point, you have two options:

- Get up off the sofa and start running around the house in a stressed state, trying to catch Fred as he pees up the walls and tears your curtains.

- Stay on the sofa and allow Fred to have a wander until he leaves of his own accord (maybe if you look at Fred, you'll notice how harmless and kind of funny he is, too).

As soon as you chase Fred around and out of the house, you increase your stress levels and make things worse: not only for you, but for Fred as well. Remember, all he wants to do is have a wander round the living room, a little sniff and then leave of his own accord.

It's your job to train your Universal Mind to stay seated on the sofa. To be present with Fred and just observe him. He's a cat. Totally harmless and guaranteed to leave a lot faster if you remain seated and don't try to get rid of him. In the meantime, just get on with watching *Strictly* on TV with a cuppa until he leaves. And each time he comes back, don't chase him. In fact, why not invite him in for a saucer of milk? Befriend him. He's just a friendly cat – until you start chasing him.

Can you relate to the cinema or Fred the cat analogies? I want you to remember them during your times of need. As my wise stepfather used to say, 'You can have anxious or down thoughts – just don't get anxious or down about them.'

So, how do you stay connected to the bit of you who's always sat on the sofa? By sticking to your 10 minutes of morning meditation, taking one to three mini-meds during the day, and crafting a lifestyle that creates the optimal amount of flow experience in your day.

Lifelong meditation

I'm normally very gentle in my teaching style, and accept that wellbeing and happiness practices can and do drift in and out of our lives like waves of energy passing through the ocean. However, the one practice I urge people *not* to skip or fluctuate on is the 10-minute mindfulness meditation performed each morning.

I'll never forget hearing Wayne Dyer relay a story about how he asked Deepak Chopra for advice on how to deal with a problem he was facing with his wife. Each time Wayne said 'Well…you see, she said she wouldn't…' Deepak interrupted with 'meditate'.

Dyer then tried to wiggle around Chopra's churlish response, saying, 'But you see, you don't understand Deepak…' to which Chopra replied 'meditate'.

This went on and on, and despite Chopra's churlish behaviour, Dyer finally *got it*. He got that we don't *really* have a problem or a stressor until we *make it* a problem or a stressor by how we, the perceiver, perceive it.

Another cool bit of wisdom relating to the fundamental importance of meditation came from Gandhi, who said:

> *'I've got twice as much on today; therefore, I'm going to need to do twice as much meditation.'*

When I first heard it, this quote blew me away because it illustrates a paradoxical truth: that *even* when you are an enlightened, driven, courageous and happy human being, you still must have the humility to maintain and grow on that path. It's a never-ending journey of spiritual awakening. Just because you were doing well observing thoughts and staying calm last week doesn't mean you can stop meditating this week.

Through personal experience and reading, I have a deeply held belief that daily meditation holds the answers to our problems because it teaches us not to find one. It teaches us to ride whatever thought wave our life presents in that moment, knowing that it too will eventually break on the shore.

Lifelong mini-meding

Alongside your sacred 10-minute morning meditation, challenge yourself to keep the mini-meds running through your day and lifetime. You don't always have to use a timer for those two minutes either, as often a mini-moment of mindfulness can happen spontaneously.

However, if you have a busy lifestyle and find yourself getting easily stressed, the structure of the mini-med is well worth retaining. The idea behind breaking up your day with observing the moment is twofold:

1. It stops you slipping unconsciously into getting up off the sofa and chasing Fred.

2. It balances your hormones from fight-or-flight mode (adrenaline) to digest and rest (serotonin).

With more calming hormones running through your body, not only are you going to feel calmer, you'll digest your meals better too. The better your digestion, the more energy you'll assimilate from your food. The more energy you have, the easier that workout will be to perform, the easier that chore will be to do, the easier that deadline will be to reach, the easier that child will be to ignore! (I could carry on if you like?) Mini-meds make life easier. Period!

Tips from your coach

Below are five further tips to assist your daily mini-med practice in the long term.

- Do it even if you don't feel as if it'll do anything to help (because the moment you don't think it's necessary is the moment it's more necessary than ever before).

- Do it even on the busiest of days. Two minutes spent on the loo in between the carnage of chores and to-do lists is as sacred as doing it on a special meditation cushion bought from a yoga website.

- Practise sending love to someone in your circle as a way of focusing your mind on something peaceful.

- Don't worry if your mind is having a particularly hectic period of thought cycles. Why they come about is almost impossible to answer conclusively. The solution, however, is always the same: breathe deeply and slowly and stay on the couch as Fred wanders around!

- To breathe is to be in spirit and to be in spirit is to breathe. No matter what's going on in your physical world, you're only one breath away from some peace in the infinite land of your divine spirit.

- Remember the slippery slope of perfectionism and the grassy path of good enough? This applies to your thoughts too. Don't be hard on yourself if you have a period of producing more anxious or down thoughts. None of us has perfectly positive thoughts in a day.

If we asked him, even the Dalai Lama might confess to having the odd negative thought. It's essential you walk on the grassy path of good enough on this one. If you're having persistently negative thoughts, they shall pass. Just be present and don't fight with them!

Lifelong flow

*'The one thing you learn about surfing is
how to operate in the present. It's really what
the surfing experience is all about.'*

GERRY LOPEZ, SURFER

Now we're going to delve into the second aspect of lifelong living in the present: flow experiences. As you learned while following the Happiness GAP programme, flow is when you're unaware of time passing because you're so engrossed in an activity; it's when your energy, mood and wellbeing are higher. That's why I wanted it in your Happiness GAP programme, and that's why I want to go a little deeper into how to achieve more of it in your life. Let's go!

Isn't it nice when you're not thinking much? Isn't it lovely when you're so immersed in what you're doing that you forget about whether life is playing fair or not? How often is the best solution to a problem *not* trying to create a solution in the first place? In just letting it be?

Much of why flow is an essential happiness ingredient lies in what it does to your brain. Studies show that people who have a flow experience get a major boost in dopamine levels, increasing their energy and focus. Not only does dopamine make you feel great, it also gives you much needed perspective and insight into any of the barriers you might be facing in your life.

If you have a financial, career or relationship problem, it's often your focus on it that perpetuates the stress and intensity. Break the cycle of trying to figure out how to solve the problem by immersing yourself in a flow experience, and often, a simple solution will present itself out of thin air. If you're the kind of person who tends to think 'what if...', flow experiences will help you shift towards 'I can see things more clearly now.'

Q&A: flow experiences

I've come up with a question and answer on what is without doubt the best natural Prozac for us humans!

Q: *I'm not getting good at the activity I want to do, and I'm not getting any flow – how long do I give it before I move on to something else?*

A: Remember, flow is achieved when our skill level is met by an equal level of challenge. If skill is too low and challenge too high, those nagging thoughts can come up as you're heavily involved in learning the skill.

Simply put, flow is about perseverance. You must be patient if you're learning a new skill and becoming frustrated that it hasn't yet become an autonomous one. When I was learning to surf, my skill level was nowhere near capable of experiencing flow. But after some persistence my skill level was met by the challenge, and whammo –

time went out the window and happiness energy went through the roof.

You must give yourself room to learn the steps involved in the activity you'd like to get better at: like a child would – gently but passionately; without self-scrutiny but with bucketloads of enthusiasm. Sooner or later, your improved skill level will allow your autonomous side to kick in, taking over thought and therefore taking over your spirit with happiness. Be patient and remember that good things come to those who wait!

Q: *What if I combined my work with flow? Wouldn't that be the real answer to a happier life?*

A: If you can experience flow in your work and be free from internalized thinking, you'll certainly be much happier. But, as you've learned while following the GAP programme, we must learn to accept what we can't control right away. Sure, you'd love to do what you love for work all day, but that might not be possible in the immediate term because following your passions takes time and effort.

Let's say you want to be a life coach, write a book and inspire people in live gigs because your moments of helping people, doing creative work and public speaking have brought you tremendous amounts of soul-enriching, body-energizing, thought-free flow. Then you set the goal of wanting more of that in your life.

If you find yourself back in your day job feeling either under- or overwhelmed by it, try to avoid adding extra pressure to your life by letting your present situation frustrate you. In a nutshell: if your work isn't what you love, don't wish you were doing something else – unless images of your wishing inspire you in that moment.

Take action towards your dream job; just don't get attached to the outcomes of that journey too tightly. When you put faith in your ability to enjoy the journey, the Universe will have a way of presenting your rewards in the right way, right on time.

Q: *I get a tremendous amount of flow in my work, but find that as soon as I leave it at the end of the day, I get all kinds of stressful and worrying thoughts about all kinds of irrational things. Is there a way of avoiding these feelings?*

A: There are a couple of things to consider here. First, it's unrealistic to expect to be in the present all the time. Sure, it makes us far happier to be in the flow of doing something we love, but we can't expect to be there all day long. In fact, it's quite normal for people to feel a little deflated and blue when they resurface from a flow experience. Nagging thoughts come back and at times these can be a nuisance.

This is where Fred the cat comes in. Once you leave your flow experience at work, allow your mind to create the thoughts it wants to create and be mindfully aware of not leaping off the sofa and trying to get rid of Fred. You don't have to learn how to control your thoughts; you just have to stop letting them control you.

The second thing to consider is whether you could break up your day with mini-meds to ease the stress your body is going through during your flow experience. Sure, it's a beautiful feeling being immersed in the moment, but the body can take a hit during the process.

Try doing mini-meds mid-morning and mid-afternoon, and see if you feel a difference when you head home after work. Remember: there's no 'right' or 'wrong' here. Just experiment, remain open-minded and most important of all, try to avoid the pitfall of being 'perfectly' happy all day (aim instead for a 'good enough' level).

Q: *I find that my job leaves me de-energized, bored and unhappy. What can I do to get more flow in the workplace?*

A: If you're underwhelmed in your job, it could be time to ask your boss if you can take on work that challenges your personal strengths a bit more. The answer will be a simple 'yes' or 'no', and if you get the 'yes', then great, you're set for a new result.

If you get a 'no', simply practise acceptance and keep your emotional river unblocked. Does this mean you'll have to put up with the unhappiness of a job you don't like? Perhaps. But accepting that will at least give you a peace that you may not have had for a while. And with some peace, you're in a better position to think clearly about how you want your future to pan out.

You can't do that if you're continually fighting with the reality of how things are. Once you've accepted that there isn't more challenging or value-orientated work available to you right now, what could you do to take the initiative and lose yourself a bit more in your job? Could you make a colleague's day with a heartfelt compliment or take a new fitness class in your lunch break to give you a mental release?

So often, we forget how much power we have to create a new life within the one we're already living. Even just declaring that we're going to increase the level of enthusiasm and gratitude we bring to the workplace can increase our enjoyment of the present moment. Look within and you'll be surprised by what you can achieve.

Q: *I don't know where to start with flow. You say that I just need to do anything that involves focus, but I'm not passionate about anything physical or creative. What can I do to create more flow?*

A: It doesn't have to be anything more than volunteering to help people in need, or reading an enthralling book. The key is putting yourself in a place where you lose yourself. The reason I recommend people do more creative and physical things is simply due to the added benefits of endorphins from exercise and satisfaction from seeing something you've created.

Creation and sports manifest wonderful physical and mental side effects, but we also get a 'high' from things like helping those in need and learning new things. Don't get bogged down in what it is that brings you flow experience. Could you write poetry? Learn a new language? Do some voluntary work in a place that needs your help?

The key is simply to challenge yourself (not too much, not too little) and enter the time-free bliss of flow as often as you can. Be disciplined about getting in your flow as often as you can, even when you don't necessarily feel like it.

Why? Well, often, we need to ask ourselves, 'Am I feeling blue because I'm not immersing myself in a challenge? Or am I just blue?' Aside from those authentic 'down' feelings that just require some acceptance, most of what we need to do to get out of a slump is probably the former.

Just get out of your comfort zone a little and think of the wise words of American writer and humorist Mark Twain: 'Twenty years from now, you'll be more disappointed with the things you didn't do than the things you did. So throw off the bowlines. Sail away from the safe harbour. Catch the trade winds in your sails. Explore. Dream. Discover.'

Balancing present joy and future excitement

*'Happiness is a delicate balance between
what one wants and what one has.'*

ANON

In a recent episode of the kids' TV show *Sesame Street*, a character called Cookie Monster, known for his voracious appetite, embarks on a spiritual journey towards better eating habits. In his movie *The Spy Who Loved Cookies*, Cookie leads a curriculum designed to teach preschoolers the importance of self-regulation and delayed gratification. Trying to curb his sweet tooth, Cookie has a new mantra: 'Me want it, but me wait.'

There's a truth in Cookie's words. If we live only for the moment and follow our primal biological impulses in the present, we can lose sight of the health, satisfaction and long-term happiness benefits of delayed gratification. At the same time, placing too much emphasis on the future can sacrifice present joy. It's about finding a happy medium.

Is a lack of balance between present and future the reason why so many rat-racers have a midlife crisis? And why so many hedonists lack good health or a sense of direction? The key is knowing who you are and what you need.

I'd like to tell you that I've found the perfect balance between living now and working towards my future, but the truth is, I get it wrong. A lot! I don't want to add further worry and frustration to your already hectic lifestyle – all I want you to do is become more mindfully aware of how you'd like to feel now, and what you'd realistically like more of in the future.

Are you on the present road or the future road?

Your quest for optimal happiness is finding that sweet spot between the present and the future. How do you know if you're in the right place? Well, that's about checking in with your intuition and energy levels. You'll know you're in the right spot when life feels good now and underneath, there'll be a deeper sense that there's stuff to be excited about in the future too.

Put simply, the career-driven person chasing the future destination could probably benefit from some present-moment awareness and, depending on how much flow their work brings them, some flow experiences too.

Likewise, the hedonistic, dessert-scoffing sofa surfer who thinks a job is something you do simply to pay the bills might benefit from some graft towards a future dream. If you're more of a hedonist, it could be a good idea to stop doing nothing about the future and start getting busy in the present. Likewise, if you're more future-driven, it could be a good idea to slow down to the present more often.

Below I've described two lifestyle scenarios; think about which one is playing out for you at any given moment. You know yourself better than anyone, so play with the following ideas and see which ones feel like the right fit for you. You can come back to them whenever your life feels out of balance.

For example, feelings of underwhelm, boredom and listlessness can creep in after the high of completing a long-term project has ended, just as feelings of overwhelm, anxiety and pressure can creep in when we've taken on too much.

The present road

In this lifestyle scenario, you sometimes feel that you're too far down the 'present road' (with a sense of lacking future excitement/satisfaction/drive/purpose). If you find it hard to sacrifice what you want to do in the present moment for future excitement, try some or all of the following ideas.

1. Create a reward-based system

If there's an activity that you have to do which will help you in the long term, but you know you won't enjoy doing it, put a reward in place for after you've completed it. Just knowing there's something cool waiting for you on the other side of your work is enough to lift your energy levels. Plus, it will increase the satisfaction and pleasure of the reward (because you've earned it).

You could watch a funny movie, eat your favourite dessert, go for a run or read for pleasure. Two of my personal favourite rewards are arranging for my family to meet me at a local café for breakfast after I've finished my writing for the morning, or giving myself a little bar of sea-salt dark chocolate after an afternoon session of work.

2. Have the reward before the 'have to' activity

Watching the funny movie or eating dessert *before* doing that thing can raise positive hormones that offset the apathy of not wanting to do it. A good mood can potentially override the boredom or difficulty you associate with the task. It can also give you a clarity you might not have had before – a clarity that might get you thinking totally differently about the task.

Here are a few more ideas; have a play and test the results.

- Be present with the pleasure you're supposed to be getting from an activity by making sure it plays to your strengths *and* challenges you (remember – flow experiences are found when you have roughly equal skill and strength to meet the demands of a challenge).

- If you *really* can't be bothered to do something, do a big sweaty workout beforehand. The rush of endorphins can make even the most boring tasks seem more interesting.

- Drink your coffee/tea with coconut oil. The oil contains medium chain triglycerides (MCTs), which have been proven to sharpen the mind and lift energy levels – and it's good for you too! (To discover more about this, check out Dave Asprey's blog 'The Bulletproof Coffee'.)

3. Manage your emotional state

One of my clients gave me a cool insight into the way we manage our emotional state when faced with difficult, time-consuming and sometimes stressful work/situations/chores. She said that if we're faced with one of these and can't seem to find a way out, we need the following:

- **The self-awareness** to notice that our lowered emotional state is only making things worse.

- **The discipline** to get off our ass and do something to 'break the state' (ideally movement/getting out in nature to bring endorphins and fresh air).

- **The ability** to see things from a **new perspective**.

Put simply, if you find yourself becoming overwhelmed by anything, at any time, leave it alone and move on to something else, or ideally, go for a workout. When your dopamine levels are low (through tiredness and stress), no amount of 'trying' to get a job done will work. Sure, you could spend five times longer on it than you normally would and finish it with sheer grit and determination, but it doesn't have to be that way.

If you're the kind of person who puts their nose to the grindstone on a project but through burnout and stress becomes overwhelmed, become more mindful of your emotional state and make sure it's a good one when you're in the moment of doing what you're doing. So often, people give up on dream projects not because the goal isn't the right one for them, but because they don't manage their emotional state on the journey to the goal.

4. Assume there's a good reason

If you've been putting something off, assume there's a good reason for it. With hindsight, you'll be able to look back and know why you put it off for so long. Don't try to work it out from where you are now – it's almost impossible without a broader perspective. You'll get too caught up in your own thinking and go round in circles.

Paradoxically, the more you try to work out why you keep putting something off, the less likely it is that you'll get on with it; over-thinking will make you feel even worse and the snowball of procrastination will continue. That's the one trait of procrastinators I seem to notice more than any other – being way too bloody hard on themselves!

Accept that there's a good reason why something's not happening right now. You don't need to work out exactly what it is right away. In fact, the more you just leave it alone, the more likely it is that a light bulb solution will present itself almost effortlessly – when you're least expecting it.

5. Give yourself permission to procrastinate

If you find yourself continually putting something off and feeling bad for it, bring your mind back to the present. If you're watching TV instead of getting on with your dream project, house chores or exercise routine, you're just watching TV. It's only when you feel guilty about not doing what you should be doing that things can turn nasty. Nobody is assessing your life anywhere near as closely as you think they are, either.

I recently heard a cool little saying, 'At 18, we care greatly what other people think of us; at 40, we no longer give a damn and at 65, we realize no one was thinking about us in the first place.' Keep that in mind if you keep putting things off, because in all truth, how much of our stress arises from what other people think about our lives? Our weight, career, love life, lifestyle, mental health or anything in between? If no one ever infiltrated our lives, would we beat ourselves up about not doing x, y or z?

Even if people *are* talking about us, how can we control that? The only thing you have control over is a choice to be kinder to yourself in the present. Enjoy the TV, enjoy the procrastination, and I hope, in a funny kind of way, you'll notice something shift within that could actually get things moving again.

6. Get to know your real self

In a month, year or few years from now, you'll probably be able to work out why you didn't act on that calling, and reset goals that genuinely inspire you to take action as you learn what intrinsically motivates your spirit.

I've seen this happen on hundreds of occasions in my coaching career – people start off with reasons for a goal being a, b, and c, only to discover the reasons for the goal aren't anything to do with a, b and c.

The better you get to know yourself, the easier it becomes to understand what really fires you up. For example, a client came to me last year looking to slim down her waistline and improve her energy levels. In our opening session, the conversation centred light-heartedly on habits and lifestyle choices, leading to *some* action towards her future. Fast-forward six months and we found out that the real reason she wanted to take action on her body was related to how she saw herself, her relationship with her husband and the kind of mum she wanted to be. Understanding her *deeper why* stoked her spirit towards a more formidable *how*, and she's now in the best shape she's been in for years.

The future road

In this lifestyle scenario, you sometimes feel as if you're too far down a 'future reward' road (and are experiencing a lack of pleasure release for the present moment). If you tend to sacrifice present joy for long-term success, either personally or professionally, experiment with these practical ideas.

1. Give yourself regular pleasure breaks

An ancient proverb says that 'the body heals with play, the mind heals with laughter and the spirit heals with joy'. If your life provides you with flow, joy, laughter and play, the need for pleasure breaks need not apply – your work and chores *are* your healers. If, however, your work isn't your passion and doesn't play to your strengths, make an effort to put pleasure breaks into your day.

It could be stopping what you're doing at work and looking at old holiday photos for 15 minutes, or leaving your gadgets at your desk and taking a relaxing stroll through the park. Plan one pleasure break for every two hours of work. Not only will the positive hormones released boost your productivity levels, they'll reduce stress as well.

If it helps, try adding your pleasure breaks to your reminders on a phone or tablet. I know how futile the pleasure break might seem from the fence of a busy schedule – when your job is stressful, taking one might be the last thing on your agenda. It's only with hindsight that you'll look back and think, *Wow, I needed that*. Trust in the future benefits, no matter how hard your day is.

2: Book fun into your diary

Experiment with adding one hedonistic activity to your diary, once a month. The smaller you start, the easier it will be to create the habit of pleasure. Over time, you can work on adding more into your life. This doesn't have to be an exact amount of fun, either. It could be a golf day with the girls or just a quick coffee and gossip with the guys (un-sexist? I thought so).

So much of our happiness comes from the build-up to something. Like the weeks leading up to Christmas, which are almost as fun as Christmas Day itself (if not more so). When something's in the diary, you'll get just as much pleasure from knowing you're *going to* have fun as doing the fun thing.

We humans often intend to do more fun things but never book them into the diary. I know that scheduling fun takes some of the spontaneity from it, but if you're a rat-racer who always foregoes the present moment for some future benefit, pleasure scheduling could be a wise move.

3. Make sure you're aligned with your values

If you value your professional life on a deep level, you don't need to explain that to anyone – especially if you're enjoying your work and getting flow from it. It's just about making sure it's aligned with your deepest values. You don't need to explain or compare yourself to anyone but you. People have opinions – each of them valid and worthy in themselves – but they're for other people to think and feel.

I recall someone in my circle getting funny with me after I'd pulled a six-hour writing session, saying it was too much for me. I can't deny the truth in her words, but when you're inspired and motivated by your work, and get flow from it, it can take you over. You can't change what people say, but you *can* change how you manage your inner compass. If, deep down, you're loving life, loving your work, loving who you're becoming, you don't need to answer to anyone but you.

I also think it's essential to remember that every person in your circle is influenced by how *you* feel. The better you feel, the better they'll feel. Sure, families can get lonely when someone's not around all the time, but any short-term longing will be outweighed by the uplifting effect a happier human has on others by doing what they love.

You needn't stress yourself thinking about balance if you can't achieve it right now. If your work makes you happy, it's far better that you bring that happiness home with you than let go of work responsibilities and become less of who you love being. If, however, you don't love your work, could it be time to start becoming the coconut-cutter you can become and yield to the challenge of living a more inspired life?

4. No matter how busy you are, stay with the moment

Person one wakes the kids, gets them ready and drops them at school; they then head to the office, work a 12-hour shift, pick the kids up, maybe squeeze in a gym session, cook the dinner, put the little 'uns to bed, and finally sit down for one hour in the evening, getting hardly any downtime. Person one doesn't feel all that stressed. Tired, but not stressed.

Person two does the same as person one but feels stressed and overwhelmed. What's the difference? Person one remains mindful of present activities and person two doesn't. Person one helps the kids in the morning on a moment-to-moment level – opening the cereal box, pouring the milk. Person one is staying *with* the moment. Person two does exactly the same activities as person one, but their mind is racing about how much they have to do that day, before the day has even taken place.

So, how do we overcome this cycle of doing one activity but thinking about how much we have left to do after we've done it? By meditating for 10 minutes on waking each morning, and mini-meding throughout the day and connecting to a higher consciousness.

Even if you have tons to do each day, it will leave you feeling much happier and less stressed to cultivate a mindset that goes *I'm here. I'm doing this activity, and when it's done, I'll move on to the next one*, rather than *OMG! I've got so much left to do after this!*

5. Fill your well at least once a day (mindfully)

No matter how hectic your schedule, stick to at least one thing that brings you present joy. It doesn't need to be spectacular, expensive or time-consuming, but it's essential you do something for your spirit each day that fills the 'well of positivity'. Does watching TV in the evening count? Sure, if you're mindfully *with* the TV. So often, we stick on the box or play with our phone as a means of distraction which, overall, doesn't leave us feeling all that relaxed or joyous.

If fiddling around on your smartphone and mindless TV-watching is what you love, that's fine. As the old saying goes, if it ain't broke, don't fix it. However, in my experience, and after my research on mindfulness and flow, activities such as playing board games, cooking a new recipe or even just watching TV shows with a higher mindful attention tends to put us 'in the moment' of flow and positive emotion far more than distraction for distraction's sake. This is something for you to experiment with.

Lifelong Living in the Present recap

▶ Will it be easy for you to make meditation a daily habit for the rest of your life? If not, aim for as little as two minutes per day with a mini-med.

▶ Become mindful of not trying to get rid of Fred the cat – chasing him will land you in a neurotic battle with your own thoughts (which only gives them more strength).

▶ What could you do to create more time-less flow in your life?

▶ How balanced are your present joy and your future excitement? If you're too far down one road or the other, what steps could you take to improve balance, and upgrade your happiness?

Happiness GAP case study

Trisha (unlucky in love, and happier)

Trisha was a successful City lawyer who came to me for life coaching and help with weight loss. When we first met, I was struck by how bolshy and quick-witted she was: on being asked to do her last of set of squats for the workout, she'd turn and say 'NO!' If Trisha didn't want to do something, you knew about it!

Initially, I found her demeanour offensive, but after a while, I grew fond of her strong attitude. Once she'd achieved her goal of losing weight, she carried on training and coaching; I imagine this was a kind of pseudo-therapy – based on the endorphins from exercise and getting to talk with a bloke who actually listened without giving solutions to her problems.

Trisha usually struggled with guys, but around a year into our time together, she found someone who managed to pass her strict testing process and make it to date #2! A few months into that relationship, though, Trisha said to me: 'I'm really struggling with Luke. He's obsessed with growing facial hair, and as for his taste in movies… Oh my God, he's like a teenager, watching so many Marvel comic films. I really don't know if I can be with a guy who doesn't share my taste for fine food and reading!'

Six weeks later, Trisha announced that her relationship with Luke was over, because as she put it, they were 'too different', and she 'just couldn't put up with it'. In the months after the break-up, Trisha trained well but remained unhappy about her love life. She told me about a few failed first dates – 'He had a beard...OMG! Who the hell wears a beard to a date?!'

Trying to be a good bloke, I simply nodded and said, 'Too bad, Trisha...maybe next time.'

Once I'd started getting results from the Happiness GAP programme with other clients, I asked Trisha if she fancied giving it a go. She agreed, but on one condition: 'I won't do anything I don't like, Will. I'll just pick and choose my way through it. I just find all that self-development stuff such bullshit at times. Is that OK?' I said it was.

A week or so into the programme, we went through some of what she'd put into practice. Writing the gratitude journal felt 'forced', she said, but she ploughed on with it anyway. She found her self-acceptance affirmations 'really hard to remember' and with so much going on in her life, 'living in the present' wasn't easy.

I was ready to accept that I couldn't help Trisha when a little spark of positive change took place towards the end of the 21 days. During one session, she said, 'I think I've figured something out that I wasn't so aware of before. I'm not very nice to myself. The more aware I've become of my thoughts and my life in general – from all the journal-keeping and mindfulness in the last few weeks – the more I've noticed how harshly I talk to myself in my own head.'

By slowing down to the moment, Trisha had tapped into a higher awareness of her own thoughts. It was the coolest thing

I've seen in my coaching career. I'd never before witnessed someone so cold become so warm in such a short period of time. Although she was still a strong character, Trisha had softened a lot – mainly in the way she spoke about others: it wasn't so harsh and she was no longer so quick to judge. It was as if the way she'd treated blokes was a reflection of how she'd treated herself.

Trisha continued with the gratitude and acceptance exercises as a way of boosting her mood. But what she couldn't live without was the presence ones, which kept her tuned in to how her own thoughts looked, felt and sounded. To her, they were a way of 'keeping the brakes on' running a self-hateful inner dialogue.

The GAP in action

G – *Trisha was happier after journaling about her thoughts each evening: 'It did more to help me get my thoughts down on paper than it did to see more of the positives in my life. And so, in a really powerful way, I'm really grateful for what the gratitude journaling has done for my silly head!'*

A – *She created some self-acceptance affirmations, but found it difficult to remember them during her times of need; she also didn't make any inspiring self-reflective changes to boost her love life. But she did manage to tap into a higher awareness of how harshly she spoke about herself, so bringing about more emotional flow.*

P – *Trisha's awareness of the present moment during her meditation sessions gave her a new appreciation of the peace contained in the breath. A peace she could always go back to any time her life threw her crap.*

Applying the Happiness GAP
to Your Relationships

*'Your friends are God's way of
apologizing for your family.'*

Dr Wayne W. Dyer

In the next two chapters I'm going to take you through how the Happiness GAP can be applied to two areas that are responsible for much of our happiness: our close relationships and our health and wellbeing. Let's go!

In 2002, two American pioneers of positive psychology, Ed Diener and Martin Seligman, conducted a study at the University of Illinois on the 10 per cent of students there with the highest recorded scores of personal happiness. They found that the most noticeable characteristics shared by students who were very happy and showed fewest signs of depression were 'their strong ties to family and friends and commitment to spending time with them'.

Better relationships = more happiness

During my research on this topic, I was blown away by the amount of literature that supports the equation, better relationships = more happiness. I was similarly enlightened after reading Danish happiness researcher Meik Wiking's *The Little Book of Hygge*, in which he says, 'In all the work I've done on happiness research, this is the point I'm surest about: the best predictor of whether we're happy or not is our social relationships.'

Have you noticed this paradigm play out in your own life? Before I developed the Happiness GAP programme, I was a little sceptical about how strong an impact our close ties could have on happiness. I was more rigid in my thoughts, feelings and actions regarding my close relationships back then. It's only with hindsight that I can see how much happier I am from applying the programme to my close relationships. Through it, I've become more grateful for them, accepting of them and present with them.

The power of applying the Happiness GAP to close relationships is most vividly demonstrated to me when I'm in the company of my mum. For years, I felt a tension between us. I had my rigid view of the world and she had hers.

On one occasion, my mum fed my daughter a food I didn't want her to eat, for health reasons. She was of the opinion that said food was OK for her and I was sure it wasn't, which I made clear, causing a row.

It's also my belief that speaking about other people's lives is neither productive nor enjoyable, but this is something my mum does, and before I filled my Happiness GAP, I was always calling her out on it. I remember once saying to her: 'Mum, you can't talk about people like that! It fills me with dread to think what you must be saying about me, if you talk about others in this way.'

It's not as if my way is 'right' either. We are both on our own unique journeys and to suggest that someone's doing something 'wrong' makes the judger just the same (if not worse) than the judged, doesn't it?

All my 'needing to be right' ever did was make things worse. It neither made Mum change nor made either of us feel good. Each time I wanted to be right, she became the person without the information while I was the person with it. The distance between us grew and grew until I realized where so much of my angst was coming from: my lack of gratitude for who she *is*, the blockage in my emotional river caused by trying to control who she *isn't*, and my inability to be present with how I wanted to choose to behave.

Maybe you have little to no difficulty with your family relationships, or have tons of trouble from the people around you – regardless of where you are in your journey, the following Happiness GAP strategies will help you achieve happier close relationships.

G – What are you grateful for in those close to you?

Practising gratitude can do wonders to heal old wounds between people. I'm not suggesting it can treat severe cases of past trauma, but I know it's beneficial for folk whose parents, teachers, peers, siblings, work colleagues and ex partners have messed 'em up a little (aka – nearly all of us!).

In the long term, continuing to feel anger or resentment towards those who are close to you for things they've done in the past is like holding a hot stone with the intention of punishing them, except you're the one who gets burned.

Yes, I know they've given you scars; yes, I know they probably hurt you; yes, I know they did x, y or z. In this life, you play the cards you've been dealt and if you want to continue playing them in favour of anger or resentment, that's totally up to you. It's just, well, you've got to see that doing so is hurting you and no one else!

Person x can be an idiot sometimes (and will probably continue to be so), but would you be who you are today if it wasn't for him or her? We have a choice. We can either blame person x or y for the way we are or decide to accept our past as been and gone and move into a more liberating future – one in which we let go of old baggage and look to grow.

Take the paralysing plight of perfectionism instilled during childhood. Sure, it doesn't help at times, and yes, walking on a sunnier path where we don't put ourselves under so much pressure would be a wise move. But perfectionism can, and often does, also create a huge amount of drive and ambition in people. It's a downside that has an equal upside – something to be grateful for.

So, how does this relate to you and your close relationships? Well, no matter what we've been given by our parents, peers, siblings and partners – no matter how much crap they've left us with, no matter how much we blame them for why we are who we are – there will be many potential upsides to the downsides.

I have a strong belief that one of our biggest quests is discovering what those positive upsides are. And then? Consciously reminding ourselves of how beneficial that is to our life today. Beginning the quest means focusing on who our loved ones *are* and what they've *given us* instead of who they *are not* and what they *haven't given us*.

Happiness GAP case study

A few years ago, I coached a woman called Lucy who was having difficulties with her sister. During one call, she said, 'I don't know what's wrong with her: she just seems so disconnected from the idea of spending time as a family, and I'm fed up.'

I asked Lucy what she was grateful for in her sister. 'Well, I can't think of anything, to be honest,' she replied. Rather than getting her to come up with something on the spot, I set Lucy the challenge of thinking carefully about what she was grateful for in her sister each evening, and then writing it down. A few weeks later, I asked her, 'Could you send a text message to Jane, letting her know how much she means to you and why?' After some 'arm round the shoulder, kick up the bum' coaching, Lucy came up with this:

'Hi, Jane: I was just waiting to pick up the kids from school, which reminded me of how helpful it was to have you help me out with them last week. And if you're going to Mum's birthday do next week, could you pick up a cake as I won't have time to get one before then?'

'There seems to be a transaction going on here,' I said when I read this. 'You're giving Jane a gratitude message that starts off beautifully, but then you ask something of her, and so it tails off on a less than inspired note.'

Lucy and I worked and worked at creating what I call a 'Pure Love' gratitude message – one that leaves both sender and receiver with a genuinely deep feeling of love – life's most potent happiness booster. If we send a gratitude text that contains our 'side reasons' for sending it, or asks for something in return, the magic evaporates because we're holding something back that can't be intellectualized. It's like a protective shield we create to stop ourselves from getting emotionally hurt.

Put simply: making your gratitude text message a one-way transaction is where you'll find the magic. Make it pure and free of side reasons, and with no motive other than to let the other person know what they mean to you and why.

And most importantly, make it vulnerable. As vulnerability researcher Brené Brown says in her book Daring Greatly: *'We cultivate love when we allow our most vulnerable and powerful selves to be deeply seen and known.'*

After some time spent working on upping the vulnerability and stripping back the layers she'd used to protect herself, Lucy came to this wording:

'Hi, Jane: Just wanted to let you know what you mean to me – how blessed I am to have you. I'm sitting here thinking about how grateful I am to have your support, love and trust. I know I can turn to you in a crisis, and for that, I'll forever be thankful.'

After sending this second message, Lucy said she hadn't felt as good in years. She'd felt true love for herself by giving true love to another. And although we'll never be able to intellectualize love, we somehow all know what it is, what it feels like, and what it means. Lucy got a bigger lift from sending the second message because she'd allowed herself to be seen – to be completely open and vulnerable in heart and soul.

That's the part of us we hide in an attempt to preserve the status quo. It's bull**** because sending a message of depth and power will never go the wrong way. You, the sender, get to feel what it's like to be vulnerable and in doing so, you re-connect to what true *love feels like. And true love can only be felt if we're our most open, honest and vulnerable – without side reasons getting in the way of what matters.*

Will most *people respond to a true gratitude message? I'd say so. Is that why you send one? Not really. Being openly grateful towards another human and wanting nothing in return will give you a rush of love through your body and soul. I guess that's all the motivation we need, isn't it?*

Gratitude didn't stop Lucy from getting frustrated with her sister every now and then. That's life. But, overall, she reported feeling significantly happier for being openly grateful. Eventually, Jane ended up gradually spending more time with the family. Was it through Lucy's actions? Who knows? All Lucy needed to know was how good it felt to tell her sister what she meant to her and why.

Gratitude exercises

Let's round off this first 'Applying the Happiness GAP' *section* with three gratitude exercises for building stronger close ties that will allow love and kinship to flourish in your life and the lives of others:

1. Say 'thank you' in a certain way

When you want to say thank you to a loved one, a co-worker, a friend or anyone in between, for what they do or have done for you, say it with an authentic tone – the kind that really gets the message through.

You see, there are two ways of saying thank you in this world: the way that says 'Thank you for your love, help and service' and the way that says 'Thank you for making my life better with your love, help and service.'

You'll know when you've hit the second one when your words make someone feel special and most importantly, needed. The more you practise saying the words with a deeper and more authentic tone, the easier it will be to repeat them next time. There isn't a single type of relationship in this world that won't benefit from this approach; people want to feel needed, not just physically, but emotionally too.

2. Notice how gossiping makes you feel

If you find that you're habitually naysaying what others are doing, ask yourself, *Is talking about person x behind his back making me feel good?* Then also ask, *Would I want people talking behind my back?* Discussing the negative aspects of the way others live their lives is a natural human habit, one that builds kinship between people in many ways. However, ultimately, it has one gigantic drawback: total loss of humility and weakening of the gratitude muscle.

The more time and energy we give to what people are not doing with their lives, the more we strengthen our mental muscles in the same direction. This makes it almost impossible to see the good people bring, which makes it almost impossible to feel the love and happiness that comes from focusing on their good points.

3. Gratitude filters out in mysterious and magical ways

How many romantic relationships could be saved if we were to show more open appreciation for one another? How many siblings would end their feuds if they said some more genuine thank-yous? How many managers would have a more productive team if they said 'I appreciate what you bring to this company' more often?

Gratitude's power to raise the consciousness of all close relationships is miraculous and magical. Just watch what happens in your relationships when you give more thanks. See old wounds heal; witness tricky communication begin to flow again; and feel the highest resonance of all from your fellow humans – one that speaks to you in ways you won't be able to describe with your head, but completely feel and understand inside.

A – Accepting others the way they are

Coming to terms with the fact that our parents, partners, siblings and colleagues are just human beings, complete with flaws (and awesomeness) is one of life's most humbling experiences.

Do you remember when the bubble burst on your view of your parents? The image you had of the awesome, giving, strong dad and mum turned more into the *occasionally* awesome, *kinda* giving, *sorta* strong dad and mum. He's a bloke. She's a lass. They each have a variety of strengths and weaknesses, but we love them all the same.

We find out that neither of them is Superman – they get hurt and also hurt others – and are kinda more like Batman. Once the bubble's burst, it's the healthy use of acceptance that helps restore the love and emotional flow to our close relationships.

Four tools to unblock your emotional river

When members of your close circle drive you up the wall, your emotional river can become blocked. Try using the following 'unblockers' to restore its flow.

1. Accept the paths of 'good enough' people

> *'We must let go of the life we had planned, so*
> *as to accept the one that's waiting for us.'*
>
> JOSEPH CAMPBELL, MYTHOLOGIST AND WRITER

Years ago, my perfectionist ways seriously harmed my relationship with my father. He was like a lot of people – flawed and full of awesomeness all at once. My pre-GAP view of the world was a more rigid one that liked to place people in labelled boxes. It meant that if my dad messed up, I lost interest and resigned myself to apathy almost instantly.

The more accepting member of our family was my sister. She was much better at accepting dad's flaws, which allowed her to still enjoy his sense of humour and incredible story-telling ability. Since his passing, I can see how much my perfectionism held me back from accepting who he was – a flawed and amazing guy.

I rarely look back and think 'what if', but if I can take one lesson I've learned since my dad's passing and aim to apply it today, it's acknowledging that the members of our close circle are never going to live up to the ideal so we should accept them for who they are – humanly flawed and infinitely beautiful.

I cringe today when I think back to how black and white I once saw the world. I can recall occasions where I'd say to my wife, 'People don't change – if a relationship ends that has to be it; people have to move on. There's a perfect person out there for everyone…so it wasn't meant to be.' Although I'm sure there was a grain of truth in my old words, most of my beliefs denied the giant chunk of wisdom I was about to learn in my own love life.

Around five years into my relationship with my wife, I almost ended it because she wasn't doing it for me in the bedroom; nor was she helping out with the bills or taking good care of her body shape or wellbeing. I'd created an image of my ideal woman, based on what my wife wasn't.

On one level, this is a worthwhile approach. How can we know what we want if we never find out what we don't want? But what I hadn't yet learned was how much *I* was at fault for creating the problems in the first place. I was walking the icy slope of perfectionism and each time my wife did something even *slightly* off, I slid down into cynicism and pessimism. This put her under even greater pressure to be the perfect wife, and sapped her ability to be the kind of person she knew she could be.

My wife wasn't the problem – *I* was. I wasn't aware of how inadequate my puny gratitude muscle, blocked-up emotional river and perfectionist attitude were for creating relationship happiness. And truth be told, I didn't yet have the courage to accept the inspired path to become the man I knew I could be. Rather than owning up to my perfectionist limitations, I hid behind the curtain of *it's everyone else's fault.*

It's only with hindsight that I can see how much happier I am with my wife since accepting the path of 'good enough'. I no longer try to find fault with who she is or what she's up to. I just allow her to grow at her own pace, leaving her feeling more loved; and in turn, that's made it easier for her to love me back. We still fight, but we're both happier accepting the tag of the good enough husband and wife.

Accepting good enough in our partners, parents, peers, co-workers or friends fills their lives and ours with a new kind of resonance. When we feel accepted, we feel loved. When we're being accepted for who we are, we feel safe, and that allows everybody's strengths to shine through. When the strengths shine through, the person who's allowing that to happen gets to feel their light and warmth.

If Jane is on good form because John is allowing her to be, it has a positive snowball effect: not only on the relationship, but on the individuals too. The feeling of growth that comes from accepting someone for who they are fills everyone's lives with more love than I can ever attempt to describe.

Tal Ben-Shahar says that 'when we embrace and accept, we communicate a different set of messages.

First and foremost, we are telling the person *I am with you. I care about you, and you can count on me.'*

And the resonance in this for you? Accepting others as good enough humans fills your spirit with love, which means you get to feel the benefits of acceptance more than anyone. Remember this when you meet with difficulty in your relationships.

2. Accept others' opinions

'Opinions are like assholes: everyone's got one.'

PAUL CHEK, HOLISTIC HEALTH PRACTITIONER

'Letting others be right', by accepting that we all see the world through different eyes, is the fastest way to happier relationships I know of. As I explained earlier, contesting what someone says or offering advice at the wrong moment turns you into the person with the information and him or her as the person without it.

All this does is cause more stress and distance between you. Even if you know you're right, the only part of you that wants to make sure they know they're wrong is your ego. Your soul doesn't understand right or wrong. It just is. Always observing. Always loving.

Accepting someone's view or way of doing something doesn't mean giving a green light to apathy either. If a loved one is doing something we don't like, acceptance gives us the release from needing to change what they're doing, which brings back peace. Our thoughts go from *I'm fed up with person x; she's an idiot and I've given up on her* to *Person x has her own struggles, as we all do. I'll be here for her if she ever needs me.* Apathy appears to keep happiness locked up like a parrot in a cage. Acceptance opens the cage and gives the parrot a fresh chance at life.

It's difficult to hold back when someone is harming themselves with habits and behaviours that we know are damaging. However, unless someone seeks our advice in writing, over the phone or in person, we must save our knowledge and wisdom for those who ask for it. It can be confusing when people complain about their situation – although it might sound as if they're seeking our advice, truth be told, they just want to be heard.

The fact that you're reading this book suggests you're on a journey of growth and, as such, have new insights finding their way to you all the time about how to live a happier life. However, I must urge you to remain steadfast in refraining from sharing those insights with people who haven't asked for them. As the ancient Chinese philosopher Lao Tzu said, 'Those who speak do not know. Those who know do not speak.'

Sure, you can say stuff to people close to you if you want to, but in my experience unless someone asks for advice, it usually makes things worse to speak out of turn. The next time someone says something that you don't agree with, let them 'be right' and say, 'I can understand why you feel that way' or 'It can't be easy going through that' or 'I know, it's bad, isn't it?'

Make a mental note of what happens over the next few weeks when you do this. I'd be surprised if you don't notice an overall increase in rapport and a decrease in stress. Don't think you're losing a part of yourself by going along with them either. Allowing others to be who they are does the exact opposite. Allowing someone the room to be themselves, without judgement, is the mark of a growth-orientated human.

If you want a life that's as rough and gritty as sandpaper, be more right. If you want a life like a cool, calm, blue ocean, let others be right.

And before we finish this unblocker, I'm not suggesting that you don't speak up when the time is right. Confrontation and disagreement are essential if there's a genuine problem in a personal or professional relationship. All I'm suggesting is that you question why you feel the need to be right on a given occasion. Is it because you genuinely want to help someone? Or is this your ego's need to be right? Consult your heart and you'll find the answers you're looking for.

3. Accept that you have only so much to give

'Life is a reciprocal exchange. To move forward, you have to give back.'
OPRAH WINFREY

As we journey through life, we find a tremendous strength and power in being able to say 'no'. A coaching client told me that she found it really hard to say no to one of her relatives. But then one day she came to a session with a smile on her face and said, 'You'd have been so proud of me, Will. I said no and I didn't feel bad about it.

'It was such a release, and I felt so much stronger and empowered for it too. People have been using me like a doormat for years. It's about time I took back control. I've got goals, Will; if I can't prioritize my time and energy, how am I ever going to be happier in myself and for the family?'

You can play out this unblocker however you like. If being consistently selfless is what gives you a deeper sense of fulfilment and purpose, by all means, keep on giving. I do, however, have a sneaking suspicion that a lot of people I meet and work with would love to be able to say no more often but don't have the courage. They are worried about being thought of negatively by others. If this is you, stop worrying about other people and accept that you only have so much to give before you need to take back.

If you're bound to keep worrying and it still holds you back, you have two options: a) accept the fact that you only have so much to give before you need to tell little white lies to preserve your wellbeing, and b) accept it might not be in your nature to say no. There comes a point when your human nature will dictate how you manage your life. Although change is perfectly possible and something we should all aspire to, sometimes you have to accept what you're capable of.

There's nothing worse than feeling like you 'have' to see people just to save face. Living behind the curtain of *I don't want to seem selfish* or *I don't want people to think I'm mean* can be avoided with some trust in yourself and accepting the need to take back.

If, deep down, someone feels 'happier' overall, week by week, month by month, by avoiding certain people, that's all the feedback they need to know they're on the right path, isn't it? It's easy to forget about the self in a world full of people worrying about what other people think. What 'self-acceptance' does is recognize the need to be authentic; to accept that we are who we are and we only have so much to give before we need to take back.

When we say no, we're saying to the Universe: 'I have limits; this is what I have available; this is what I value; this is what I will not do and this is how I will choose to act.' As the Buddha said, 'You can search throughout the entire Universe for someone who is more deserving of your love and affection than you are yourself, and that person is not to be found anywhere. You, yourself, as much as anybody in the entire Universe, deserve your love and affection.'

Acceptance exercise

Let's now use reframing to help you see your nature through a more positive lens: in the context of saying 'yes' too often, this *could* be perceived as a strength rather than a weakness. Play with the following examples to come up with your own 'reframes'.

Situation: You keep saying yes to a relative, friend or colleague (*when you really want to say no*), leaving you feeling drained and overwhelmed.

Reframe: You're just a really kind, compassionate and driven human being (*a positive strength*).

On the flip side, you could reframe your way out of the guilt that might come with saying no:

Situation: You say no to preserve your wellbeing and help prioritize your energy and happiness (*but it makes you feel guilty*).

Reframe: You're just a very happy individual who wants to stay that way (*a positive strength*).

If you're in the 'saying yes' camp but would *really* like to be saying no more often – because your diary is so jammed you don't have any time to recharge – then it's worth asking yourself the following questions:

- 'Am I saying yes because I'm worried about what people would think if I said no?'

- 'Would I be happier if I didn't have to spend so much time with person x or y?'

- 'Do I have evidence to back these ideas?'

If you're in the 'saying no' camp and would like to become more compassionate and giving of your time to others, then perhaps it's worth asking yourself the following:

- 'Am I allowing person x to affect me more than they should?'

- 'Are there ways I could become more compassionate/ empathetic towards person x?'

- 'Are there situations in which a few more 'yeses' here and there would make other people happier? Could I use their happiness to boost my own?'

---

4. Accept your authentic self

'Always be yourself, express yourself, have faith in yourself; do not go out and look for a successful personality and duplicate it.'

BRUCE LEE

I think there probably isn't a single point in life when you suddenly feel as if you're being your most 'authentic self' – when your thoughts and feelings are reflected harmoniously by your actions and behaviour. It's a step-by-step process that can feel awkward and slow at times. Like most things in life, it's usually hindsight that acts as a reference point for growth and learning.

Right now ask yourself: 'Am I like I was when I was younger?' Unless you're from outer Mars, my guess is that your answer will be anything from 'a bit different' to 'completely different'. But why is this important to your happiness? In order to answer that, I'll tell you my wife's journey towards her authentic self.

The Garden of Authenticity

In her twenties, my wife had friendships she'd developed at school and university, and considered those people her best mates. She had a showbizzy, ego-driven, 'gotta be seen in the right places' kind of lifestyle, but increasingly, the more time she spent going to bed early, getting out in nature and living a simpler life, the less her old life appealed to her.

Things came to a head one night after she arrived home from a party. She'd felt totally alone there, despite being among her best friends, she told me. 'I felt so insecure… I'm just so different now… there was so much pressure to drink and I just didn't want to. It's not me and they made me feel terrible for it.' I'd rarely seen her so upset.

After a good night's rest, she reflected on what she'd learned from the experience, and that inspired her to come up with the concept of 'The Garden of Authenticity' – a place we discover as we 'grow' up.

You see, when we're young, we form a persona, a mask that enables us to fit in and get along with others. The persona we create is no big deal, until we reach the inevitable crossroads in life, and have to decide whether to keep up the self that needed to fit in or continue growing into the real personality we discover in each new moment walking through our Garden of Authenticity.

My wife had grown into her true, authentic self and in doing so, had discovered parts of her Garden she didn't know existed. Being in the new part of her Garden felt calmer and happier to her. When she went back to her old lifestyle of drinking and late nights every now and then, it was as if she didn't know where she was. On the outside, she seemed totally at ease, dressed up to the nines and dancing in fancy clubs, but on the inside? Totally lost.

This example represents the importance of accepting your authentic self as a means of achieving *authentic* happiness – the kind that doesn't need to look spectacular on Facebook, as long as it feels good to you. When you accept your true self and act on it, it'll seem weird, and may frighten and confuse some people who've always known you. Some of your old circle will find it hard to understand or appreciate the change because they have a vested interest in keeping you in a box marked 'you'.

Why? Well, probably because people are generally scared of living authentically in case their peers, parents or partners criticize their new decisions. Which means when they see *you* do it, rather than bravely and introspectively ask themselves what *they* want from life and act on *their* intrinsic values, they hide behind the curtain of cowardice and jealousy in the form of criticism and naysaying.

Accepting your real self will unleash in you a huge boost in happiness. I don't know all the keys to success, but I *do* know the key to failure is trying to please everyone! Jeez, if you're living even half a life, it's going to get people talking! You can't live your life pretending to be someone you're not; it's just too much effort and, besides, your true nature is the most attractive, appealing and enthralling thing about you.

Let's round up this final 'unblocker' with six little ways to tend to your Garden of Authenticity.

Acceptance exercise

As you journey through your Garden of Authenticity and discover parts of it you love, you'll notice that, in order to help grow those parts, the weeds that block the progress of that growth need to be removed.

1. If you can't seem to grow out of spending time with people you don't want to spend time with, stop texting or calling them back. You don't have to be blunt, just accept the need to be assertive. Failing that, make up little white lies (you don't have to feel guilty about something that will make you happier in the long run).

2. Trust in the Universe. The happier you are, the more you're going to attract the same. Be patient and the right friends, lovers and clients will show up in the right place, right on time.

3. Keep consulting your intuition. If someone feels right to you, treat him or her like gold. But try to avoid becoming needy; just treat them with respect and dignity. Be openly kind and complimentary about how much you appreciate their company/business. Good rapport is built on 'I appreciate you'.

4. Notice if you're letting the idea of how your life 'should be' get in the way of living with how it really

is. It's a strange irony that the people who crave other's approval the least end up getting it the most frequently, and those who crave it the most get it the least. If you want more influence in this world, don't act cool. *Be* cool.

5. Don't fear solitude. Often, the happier we become in our own skin, the happier we are spending time alone. Lovers, clients and friends can come and go in this life, but there's only one person who's seen it through all the bits in between – little ole you. Get to love your own company and you'll grow in ways I can't begin to describe.

6. Consider the one to five really close friends you get to see every now and then and ask yourself, 'Is that a good enough amount of time with them?' Given the time and energy demands of modern life, would it be wise to evolve from a 'perfect' social life to one that's good enough?

   Play with this one in your lifestyle and notice what comes up for you. If you feel happier for accepting a good social life as 'good enough', that's great! Keep practising being more realistic in this way and reap the rewards! If, however, you don't feel happier going down this road, what could you do to make a change? Become better organized? Or maybe loosen your grip on needing a perfect social life?

P – Be mindfully present with others

For 99.9 per cent of the time, my wife doesn't need a coach-hat-wearing, solution-orientated husband. She just needs her husband. Nurturing a better relationship with my wife is a double-winner. I feel better for making sure I'm present with her, and she feels better for having someone who's hearing her words. So if you're a babbling brook of words and rarely listen to others, it could be time to 'be' with people more.

While in conversation with someone, if we're simply waiting to voice the things we want to say, that isn't being present with them – it's being with our thoughts. And, boy oh boy, isn't human intuition a beautiful thing for picking this up when we're in the company of others? How do you feel when you're not being fully listened to? It's a complete turn-off, isn't it? So, remembering how crappy it feels not to have someone with us in mind and spirit is the prompt we need to do the exact opposite.

Sure, it can be brutally difficult to keep our mouth shut when someone's being overly negative or chatting about something we don't agree with, but we must *allow them to be*. This is an often overlooked ingredient of building trust and influence.

Why? Well, we'd all love our words to inspire hope and understanding in those we meet, right? We'd all love what we say to hit the right note each time and create positive influence, but is it realistic to expect that of ourselves? A far simpler way to create long-term influence is learning to be more present with people.

As carers, leaders, parents, managers and motivators, we place a lot of pressure on ourselves when we expect our communication to be so effective and inspiring that it gets through every time. The 'doing-ness' of communication is thinking of things to say to help move others and, be truthful with yourself now, how often do those words make others do exactly what you want them to?

If you find your results are average to poor at best, it could be time to ask more questions and listen, leading to a deeper trust and kinship in your close relationships. As Stephen R. Covey, author of *The Seven Habits of Highly Effective People*, said, 'Trust is the glue of life. It's the most essential ingredient in effective communication...the foundational principle that holds all relationships.'

Before we go any further, I think it would be outlandish to suggest that any human being can be perfectly present with all people at all times, listen to what they're saying, and remain mindful of not telling them what they're doing is 'wrong' or 'bad'. What isn't outlandish is the idea that we could all become a little better at being present with people in our circle – without our opinions or smartphones getting in the way of good old-fashioned lovingness.

Happiness GAP case study

During a surfing trip, a friend and I had to carry our surfboards and wetsuits to a spot at the end of an incredibly long beach. Suddenly, worn down by heat and dehydration, I said to myself, Screw this! I'm getting in the water now. I can't handle this walk any more, *and stopped walking.*

This threw my friend off a little, and I could see he was frustrated that I'd stopped earlier than he'd wanted to. I immediately apologized for being selfish and told him my reasons for stopping sooner than planned, to which he didn't reply and just carried on walking up the beach.

This was a friend with whom I hadn't spent more than a few hours before the trip. We were on day four and, as I'm sure you can empathize from spending any length of time with people, our personalities had started clashing like frustrated pedestrians bumping into one another during rush hour.

I followed him up the beach to where he was getting changed, and apologized again. But he wouldn't engage with me and simply looked at the ground as he pulled on his wetsuit. Clearly, I'd annoyed him but he wasn't wanting, willing or able to show it.

I kept pressing him, saying, 'Mate, I really am sorry. I know I can be an idiot and selfish at times.' To which he replied, 'Honestly pal, don't worry. Let's just get in the surf.' This did little to resolve the situation (at least for me). My friend was still quiet and tense. I was still nervous and guilty.

After badgering him to open up about his feelings, he finally told me his reason for being quiet: 'Will, I'd rather just deal with it myself, mate. Honestly, when I have frustration or anger, I don't like it to get the better of me, and I didn't want to say things at that time that I didn't mean or want to say.'

My friend either didn't want confrontation or he didn't want to confront his true feelings (or both). There was nothing wrong with his way of dealing with emotion; it was just something I'd never encountered before. For the rest of our holiday together, I noticed he wasn't able to have any emotion that wasn't 'happy'. As soon as the conversation got deeper or introspective, he turned it to other matters.

To stop any inner tension I felt towards him or our relationship, I became more present with my own thinking and allowed him to be. Each time I unconsciously started letting my mind (and ego!) drift towards thoughts like, He's totally disengaged with emotion. I don't know how I can spend the next few days with him. I really should start talking about our situation, *I caught myself, laughed a little at how stupid my ego was being, and changed my focus to the view and just accepting him the way he is.*

My way of managing a relationship is very much about making sure everybody's emotions are made clear, so all parties involved can know where they stand. In my experience, this leaves people secure in the knowledge that we're all moving in the same direction. It starts kind of awkwardly, goes a little deep and tearful and ends up very huggy (and it's NOT everybody's cup of tea!).

In being more present with my friend, and not with my own thoughts about him, I noticed the tension between us ease off.

The key point in this story is the part about how being more present comes from appreciating how differently other people manage themselves, and why doing more to make them more like you will accomplish the reverse. Rarely will we ever change another person's habits, opinions or actions with our words.

Sure, it's a neat bonus if they see the wisdom in how we approach things, but surely a peaceful relationship is more important than one in which we constantly try to get somebody on our side? Something as simple as being more present with your own thinking in relation to other people could be enough to give you a wider perspective: one in which you go from thinking *I wish they'd just stop saying that* to *Our peace is more important here.*

Think back on the people in your life who have been successful, happy, healthy and maintained great relationships. Were they good at being present with others? Think about the people you love, and look up to the most – are they good listeners who allow others to be themselves? Those who're able to listen and be present have their *I need to be right to be safe* ego firmly tucked beneath their *I don't need to be right* spirit, and seek nothing but peace and happiness.

Presence exercise

Now at this point, you might be thinking something like *You don't get it, Will – when people are out of line or wrong, I have to speak up; they need to know!* In response, I want to take you through three levels of communication interpretation that will help you determine whether *to listen or speak* when talking with others.

1. In general conversation

This is a no-brainer. Just *listen* with your whole spirit. Really be with the person in that present moment and put your bleeping mobile phone on silent.

2. When they're telling you about their problems

First, listen without interrupting. Maintain eye contact (not too much, not too little) and use an empathetic, sympathetic tone when responding. If you think you have a fix for their problem, it could be time to rein in your ego.

Remember, nine times out of 10, offering a solution turns you into the person 'with' the information and them into the person 'without' it. If, on the other hand, they come asking for your advice, give them the world the way you see it, with all the coins of wisdom you have.

3. When they niggle you on a fundamental level

If you believe that in the long term, their niggling will jeopardize the strength and integrity of your relationship, it could be worth going through the short-term struggle and awkwardness of 'having it out' to seal the crack.

Tip: Don't make it *you versus them*. Bring your words back to how you feel in the general context of things. Keeping your emotions to a minimum involves remaining present with your breathing and where you take your words; take long, calming breaths and keep your words related to you, how you feel and the context. There may still be tears and emotional discomfort, but in the long-term, it could be one of the most important things you ever do.

4. When they niggle you on a superficial level

Welcome to life, my fellow human! We all made it out of the womb and here we are. The differences we have with each other will be around for good, and the key ingredient here is to remain present with your spirit and let the person be right, do their thing and roll how they roll without needing to 'get your bit in' to satisfy your ego's need. Plant your spirit the way a boat builder would plant a mast in a yacht – in the middle – strong enough to deal with all kinds of winds, waves and turbulence.

Applying the Happiness GAP recap

G – What could you say in writing that could improve the quality of your close relationships in the long term? Focusing on someone's positive traits strengthens your mind towards those positives, making it easier to love and appreciate them. Remember that energy goes where attention flows, so the more time you spend in appreciation of others, the more often you get to feel good too.

A – What do you have to accept about your loved ones? Cultivating a 'good enough' approach eases the pressure on them, which will help improve your close ties. The less you scrutinize others' mistakes, the more accepted and loved they'll feel.

Remember the unblockers:

1. Accept good enough relationships (not perfect).

2. Accept that everyone has his or her opinion and ways of doing things.

3. Accept that you can only give so much before you need to give back.

4. Accept your true self (tend your Garden of Authenticity).

P – Are you really *with* people when in their company? Practise being more present with others and see what happens in your relationships. If you ever find yourself in a state of tension with someone aim to listen to them without judgement and watch as peace returns.

Happiness GAP case study

Catherine (lacking 'me time', and happier)

Catherine was a stay-at-home mother of two who was struggling to keep up with the competing demands of caring for her children, doing household chores and being a good wife to her husband. She started coaching with me because she wanted more 'me time', and to regain some of the balance that's lost with being a full-time mum.

Catherine had read lots of articles about mums who felt so much happier after joining a yoga class or meeting up with friends for a coffee while the kids are at school. But no matter how much she tried, there was simply too little time, money or energy to do anything like this for her 'self'. To make matters worse, she found it increasingly difficult to be the kind of wife she wanted to be for her husband. She was barely able to get through a page of her book at the end of the day, let alone contemplate sex.

At first, Catherine was a little sceptical about taking on the GAP programme; but she decided it was worth a shot, as it didn't take up much time or cost any money. Two weeks into the programme, we reviewed her gratitude journal. One entry read:

'I'm so thankful for the kids…it was lovely being present with them this afternoon. I wasn't thinking about which chores I had left; I was totally in the moment with them, and their beauty really struck me for the first time in a long while!'

She went on to describe how much happier she felt for appreciating what she already had. As she said during a session: 'I've gone from thinking that looking after the kids on my own sucks and so does my life, to thinking that the chores still suck but, overall, I know how lucky I am. What I have is a huge blessing in my life.'

The GAP programme helped Catherine manage the challenges of life as a young mum. Juggling chores and childcare was still stressful, but that didn't have to mean her life was too much to handle. She was beginning to harness the power that gratitude has to build the strength necessary to deal with life's knocks and bruises.

Although Catherine's strengthened gratitude muscle was helping her deal with the stress of being a mum, she still found it hard to accept the way she saw herself as a wife, and struggled to get any 'me time' during the day. However, rather than trying to free up more time or money for her to do more of what she wanted, we decided to leave things as they were for a time, accept the situation and see what happened.

Catherine immediately felt happier for it. Why? Because she was no longer mulling over the things she couldn't change in the moment-to-moment of her life. It turned out that much of the blockage in her emotional river came not from lack of 'me time', but from comparing how much she had with that of the other mums in the neighbourhood. Once she noticed this, each time she thought of Tina, who got to play tennis three mornings a week, she loved herself enough to accept it and let it go.

It wasn't easy at first – she admitted she would much rather play tennis than wash dirty sheets, peel vegetables and do the ironing – but simply accepting the way her life was, enabled Catherine's emotional river to flow once more.

And the coolest part? Accepting her life and comparing herself to others less, boosted Catherine's happiness and gave her the lift she needed to resume her old hobby of drawing, which she fitted into the 20 minutes she had spare before picking up the kids from school.

She was also more mindful of being present with her chores. While she was ironing, she was with the ironing (and not letting herself get upset about wanting to do something else). So much of her stress had arisen from being where she was (ironing), but wanting to be some place else (playing tennis like Tina!).

Was doing the ironing in this way as exciting and uplifting as playing tennis? According to Catherine, that's a big fat 'no'! But was it as stressful and draining as it used to be? Apparently not.

Catherine also saw her relationships improve too. Previously while picking up the kids from school, her mind had been on the next day's chores. But now she was listening to what they had to say and noticing how being present and mindful of 'now' not only made her a better mummy, it also made her feel more relaxed, knowing her kids felt heard. Her happier mood and higher energy level made her feel sexier and more confident too. I won't go into detail, but let's just say Catherine's husband became a lot less grumpy!

The GAP in action

G: *Catherine was happier for writing down in her journal what she* already had *in her life; this helped her better deal with the time and energy demands of being a mum.*

A: *She was also happier after accepting her current lifestyle; this freed up her mind enough for her to get inspired about what she* could *change.*

P: *She was calmer and therefore happier for being more mindful of the present moment; this helped her perform just one task at a time (instead of letting her mind wander into how much she had left to do).*

Applying the Happiness GAP to Your Body and Mind

*'Beauty is in the eye of the beholder
and it may be necessary from
time to time to give a stupid or
misinformed beholder a black eye.'*

Miss Piggy

As a personal trainer, on thousands of occasions I've witnessed a client come through the doors of the gym at 11 a.m. with stress and negativity, and leave with contentment and a sense of perspective at 11:45.

Why is this? Well, exercise produces endorphins – feel-good chemicals that help increase our energy, alertness and positive emotion. Can a workout, followed by a fresh salad, solve *all* of your problems? Unlikely. Will a consistently healthy diet, lifestyle and exercise programme increase your self-esteem, energy and wellbeing, and help build up your resilience to life's ups and downs? Without question.

Whether you're health and fitness conscious already, not at all, or somewhere in between, applying the GAP to your body and mind is a way of feeling good for no good reason. Feeling vital because you're taking good care of your body is free, and yet, nothing could feel more valuable.

As Gandhi said, 'It is health that is real wealth, not pieces of gold and silver.' Let's now look at how you can apply the Happiness GAP to improve your health and wellbeing.

Managing your mind-body-happiness levels

It's easy to become overindulgent and lazy. I haven't escaped that trap and I don't think I ever will. More times than I'd like to admit, my body wants movement and my mind wants my lazy ass to stay seated.

My body wants to run a tight ship, you know? To feel light, fresh and ready for anything – no loose ends – and my mind wants to run all over the tight ship, throwing everything upside down in a *screw the tight ship, I wanna have fun* kind of way.

It's a jostle between what my body will want down the road and what my mind wants now. A modernized and socialized, I'm-too-healthy-to-eat-that delayed gratifier versus a less evolved and hedonistic, give-me-more-cake animal!

We can't get annoyed or upset with ourselves when we do overeat or undertrain because these tendencies are simply part of our DNA. As we evolved, we fasted and feasted and only moved when it was necessary.

A caveman spin class might have socialized the aggressive ones in the tribe, but it would've been deadly. Burn up 654 calories in 60 minutes and you would have been dicing with death; those 654 calories might have taken two weeks to find again.

You needed body fat. It was your lifeline. No one knew where the next meal was coming from, so to spin your legs round and round to 'burn fat' would literally have 'burned your lifeline'. It wasn't until humans invented agriculture that the idea of 'burning fat' was allowed to take off, and although we've evolved in many ways since then, our *I must eat everything I can because I don't know where the next meal is coming from* system is still set up in the same way.

If food is rich in calories, your DNA sees that as a good thing, which makes it moreish. So how do we disregard the battle with our DNA and do what will make our bodies feel and look the way we'd like them to? The answer is to stay free from battling with your DNA in the first place. And before you tell me you'd turn into the size of a house if you didn't 'fight' with your weight and wellbeing, let me explain.

Willpower sucks

Saying to yourself *Right, that's it: as of Monday, I'm going to avoid eating sugar, fat and alcohol for 30 days to boost my wellbeing and happiness* will likely tip you into the same habitual negative loop that made you gain weight in the first place. As soon as we tell ourselves what we can't or won't have, the sugar, fat and alcohol will always be somewhere in our mind.

The more time we spend thinking about what we shouldn't be having, the more our willpower is tested. After a few days, weeks or months of 'being good', most humans break the diet. Using willpower as our source of wellbeing is like using a credit card as our source of income. It works for a while, until we realize it's not real or remotely helpful to our long-term future.

It's one of the root causes of yo-yo dieting. No matter how beneficial or 'nonrestrictive' a diet's marketing campaign claims it is, *any* type of calorie restriction will probably rebound. Diet companies would go bust if they worked. I've got nothing against diets per se; I just believe there's a more effective way to journey through life – by managing your body-mind-happiness levels.

So, let's take a look at how you can apply the Happiness GAP to your body, not only to get it in the shape of your life, but also to enjoy abundant energy levels so you can keep on thriving right to the end. Let's go!

G – What do you have to be grateful for in your body?

We spend so much of our lives criticizing our own appearance, it becomes a habit. Instead, the next time you look in the mirror, notice what you *like* about your appearance. Is it your eyes? Hair? Smile? Curvy shape? Legs? Arms?

No matter how hard it might be in the beginning, focusing on what you like about your appearance will strengthen the brain's synapses to *see* more of the good, more of the time. As you strengthen your gratitude muscle towards what is nice about the way you look, you'll reinforce your worth and confidence.

Years ago, I was training a woman who was overweight but very happy in her own skin. Apart from teaching me to banish many of my prejudices about being overweight, she taught me the importance of gratitude and positively focusing on what we love about our bodies and lives.

She was in a loving relationship and had great fitness levels. Not only did she bust down the door on the body shape = confidence paradigm we often become fixated by, she also highlighted the importance of a strong gratitude muscle for a healthy sense of self-esteem. Put simply, if you're living a life of joy and happiness, you don't need to explain your Friday night crisps, wine and chocolate to anyone! Period! Living a healthier life doesn't guarantee happiness; it just improves your chances.

If you're quite happy eating, drinking and living the way you are, you don't have to get caught up in the 21st-century wave of *I really ought to...* just because the front cover of magazines tells you so. Ignore the naysayers and critics. Let go of what other people think, because getting involved in their business is, well, their business.

This is about *your* individual feelings, priorities and goals, not someone else's. If you feel wonderful living the way you're living, just keep living that way and be grateful for how happy you are doing so.

Gratitude exercises

I've written these three exercises for putting gratitude at the forefront of the way you manage your body.

1. Notice the good bits

Look in the mirror and identify the parts of your body that you like. Pick one area and focus on that for a week. Then pick a second area and focus on that for another week. And so on.

Keep reinforcing what's beautiful about your appearance and you'll not only raise your self-esteem, you might notice yourself turning down offers of cake or wine. Why? Well, the more positive you're feeling about yourself, the more likely it is you'll want more of the same (and vice versa).

2. Keep the 'rule of three' in your mindset

If you ever find yourself feeling blue about your body, use the 'rule of three'. Which three things are you grateful *not* to be experiencing in your body right this second? Here's an example:

1. I'm grateful that my right knee isn't sore.

2. I'm grateful that my back isn't aching.

3. I'm grateful that my hips are moving smoothly today.

It doesn't matter what it is – in fact, the more playful you make it, the more it could help break your lowered emotional state with a much-needed chuckle. Each day that you get to enjoy a myriad of pain-free areas in your body is another day to make a blessing out of them.

3. Be thankful for how far you've come

In our pursuit of a never-ending horizon, how often do we slow down and take stock of how far we've come in our journeys of healing, wellbeing and happiness? Or consider how many negative habits we've replaced with positive ones over the years?

Can you remember a time when…

*   You saw yourself, your body and your image much more harshly?

*   You'd binge on alcohol or sweets every night and wake up feeling like crap?

*   You didn't want to get naked because you felt too low in confidence?

*   You were so closed off from the idea of change that you wouldn't have even read a book like this one?

Note these things down in your journal, and feel thankful for how much you've grown as a person. Reminding yourself of what you've already achieved in life and how much you've grown is a cool little way of keeping a perspective on what you're striving for.

A – Can you accept your body and health?

What, at least for now, can you accept about your body and your health habits? You might have areas you don't like and don't want, but if you're going to make a change, the only way it'll happen is by accepting your situation for what it is right now.

Each time your thoughts drift to what you don't like about your appearance or your health habits, notice how you're speaking to yourself and choose a kinder way – treat yourself like you would your best friend.

If you have a lapse and forget to accept – ending up feeling crappy about your body and health – give yourself permission to be human. We *all* have hurtful feelings towards ourselves from time to time. The key to the healing process is giving yourself permission to feel what you feel – to be accepting of the reality of things and keep that emotional river flowing.

As your journey moves up and down, side to side, remember the words of the Chinese philosopher Lao Tzu: 'Life is a series of natural and spontaneous changes. Don't resist them; that only creates sorrow. Let reality be reality. Let things flow naturally forward to whatever way they like.'

So, if your reality is that you are the weight you are and you can't seem to shift old habits, don't beat yourself up for *what is*. I mean, can you imagine a female gorilla getting upset that she's carrying a few extra pounds from feasting on early-season bamboo? Choose a kinder way and feel an emotional flow return.

Earlier, I explained that in the long term, acceptance works on two levels: one in which you accept now for 'what is' and a second in which you accept you have the potential for the inspired path (which, in this case, is improving or maintaining your wellbeing regime).

Well, you can only get on the inspired path if you accept where you are right now. It's as if acceptance of what is unleashes the inspiration for 'what is yet to be'. If you ever find yourself stuck with your food and exercise regime, notice how much of the lack of inspiration is coming from blockages in your emotional river.

It won't be the bad meals or laziness causing the problem, but more the emotional turmoil and guilt attached to the problem that's causing the blockages. If you're watching TV instead of out running, you're just watching TV. It's only when guilt sets in that you start to cause a blockage in the flow of the river, and it's emotional flow that's going to help you get from where you are now to where you want to go.

Happiness GAP case study

A client called Cam was struggling to achieve his personal health and relationship goals. During one phone session he said, 'I don't know what's wrong with me. I'm pretty messed up really; I come out with all these things I wanna do with my life but I never actually get on with them.'

'I wouldn't worry, pal: we're all pretty messed up in our own unique ways,' I assured him.

'Yeah, but you know that goal of eating healthily for 18 out of 21 meals, healthy weekends and doing two to three workouts during the week? I haven't done any of that! I ate crappy sandwiches each day for lunch and only did one workout! And, to add insult to injury, I'm missing my targets at work. I usually make 80–120 calls in a week and I've only been managing 40!'

'Here's the thing, mate,' I replied. 'During our time together, you've mentioned how much you want to achieve and have in life, and I want you to have whatever it is you want to have. But, here's my question – do you ever give yourself a break from aiming at spectacular, incredible, awesome days? Do you ever allow yourself two 'good' weeks? Do you ever accept good as good enough?'

'You've gotta be kidding me!' Cam exclaimed. 'How am I going to be happy if I don't push towards my goals?'

'Sure…but can you see how the pressure you're putting on yourself to perform is affecting the performance?'

After several more calls, we got to the bottom of Cam's issue: he was setting unrealistically high targets for himself (aka, walking the icy slope of perfectionism). So, over the next few weeks, we adjusted his standards a little to see what would happen. Instead of three workouts in the week, one became 'good enough for now'; instead of 80–120 calls in the week, 30–50 became 'OK'; and instead of 18 out of 21 meals being healthy, 10 became 'cool for now'.

By accepting his situation and good as 'good enough', Cam restored the flow in his emotional river. He noticed how much friendlier he was being to himself for setting more achievable targets. If he didn't get something done, rather than beat himself up, he accepted the situation and moved on.

In the end, he found the increase in his overall wellbeing nudged him towards more happiness and success in his job, exercise, and health. Acceptance not only allows you to feel at peace with the natural order of things, it can also give your butt a giant push in the right direction.

Three tools to unblock your emotional river

The following three acceptance 'unblockers' will restore your mind-body-happiness and also raise your energy levels, making it easier to peel and chop those veggies and get your butt moving!

1. Forgive yourself each night

> *'Forgive yourself for not having the foresight to know what now seems so obvious in hindsight.'*
>
> JUDY BELMONT, MOTIVATIONAL SPEAKER

Whether it's a relationship you knew wasn't good for your self-esteem, food and exercise choices that have led to low energy and a slow metabolism, or just plain old negative self-chatter about the way you look, you may have made some errors along the way. Before you go any further, forgive yourself for them now and forgive yourself for them each night.

Whatever you tell yourself about who you are today, forgive and accept yourself. You made those decisions based on the best of what you had *at that time*. All you need to know about your past is that it had to happen to make you the person you are today. Without forgiveness there is no love and without love there is no happiness, and without happiness there is less natural inclination to choose loving food and lifestyle choices for yourself. It's one giant, self-fulfilling loop.

2. Accept good as good enough

> *'Every cell in your body is eavesdropping on your body.'*
>
> DEEPAK CHOPRA

Would home-cooked organic meals, consistently early nights, good hydration, five workouts a week, time spent in nature and mindful awareness throughout the entire day make you a healthier and happier human? Without question. Is a perfect level of consistency in doing this realistic? Probably not. There's nothing wrong with aiming at perfect; it's just that, normally, it leads to more frustration than it should when we slip.

Take sleep for example. If you've had a bad night's sleep, leaving you grumpy the next day, you'll be tired. But it's when you have thoughts like *How am I going to cope, being this tired?* that you ramp up the pain more than you need to. On its own, tiredness is just tiredness. Sure, you'll get less done on those days and that's why it's essential you aim for good – but not perfect – health. It gives you wiggle room for the natural ups and downs we all face in our day-to-day lives.

3. Accept the challenge

> *'Winners take imperfect action whilst*
> *losers are still perfecting the plan.'*
> TONY ROBBINS

If you want to change the shape and feel of your body, accept rather than deny yourself the challenge of doing so. If your past has taught you the powerful happiness-boosting benefits that come from enjoying superb health, it's time to jump back on the horse. Even if you simply have some inkling it would make you happier to be healthier, you're part of this challenge too.

The feeling of abundant health is certain to feed into every area of your life, including your relationships, the success and longevity of your career and your mental wellbeing. If you can accept the challenge into your life and declare that each day you'll turn up to work out, stretch, prepare home-cooked meals, get to bed on time, rise early, stay hydrated, meditate daily, and get out in nature as often as possible, come rain or shine, you, my friend, will have Gandhi's 'real' wealth – your health!

P – Are you *with* your meals?

Can you trace any of your overeating to being unconscious about stuffing your mouth with another mouthful, or snacking 'on the go'? Can you trace fluctuations in your weight to being unconscious about saying 'yes' to the offer of food and drink with friends?

When you keep your phone and TV turned off, sit and really 'be' with your food, you'll notice a tremendous shift in how much more you enjoy the meal (which often leads to smaller portions as you need less to feel satisfied).

Remember what it means to eat a meal: it's designed to nourish your body and give you pleasure. Seeing food as your friend is about becoming really present with the most authentic part of who you are – the part that doesn't need to stress about what it has or hasn't eaten. Let's now look at how being more present can have a really positive impact on your self-image, wellbeing and health.

Five tools for mind-body-happiness presence

Applying the Happiness GAP to your food/exercise/ lifestyle will not only get you from where you are to where you want to be with less effort than ever before, you'll probably be a lot happier for it too! To round up this GAP-applied chapter, let me take you through five 'present waves' to increase your mind-body-happiness.

1. Presence isn't about avoiding naughty food

Many people I've worked with beat themselves up about the way they used to live – fretting about how much it affects their health and waistline today. Likewise, many people I've worked with worry endlessly about the impact their food and lifestyle choices are having on their future.

And, to be completely honest, the GAP hasn't cured many of them of making poor health decisions. But what it has done is help many people become happier *despite* making those decisions. Applying present moment wisdom to mind-body-happiness is about turning the question from 'What won't make me fat?' to 'Am I present with this food?'

This approach cuts right to the heart of the matter. If someone is present while eating, it doesn't matter whether the food is a fourth slice of chocolate fudge cake or a lean chicken salad, the decision is a *conscious* one. If it's a conscious decision, why change?

If, however, someone doesn't feel good, and their stressed-out, calorie-passionate inner caveman/woman is making all kinds of unconscious food decisions, it's time to start experimenting with new approaches. I know this might seem overly simplistic, but in a world overflowing with analysis, I strongly believe it's never been more important to simplify our body goals and go back to *our own* wisdom!

2. Lovability is a present-moment decision

Regardless of your body shape, if you're a positive person and forgive yourself, you'll feel love for yourself. The more love you feel for you, the easier it is for someone else to love you too. Those seeking love from someone else are in for the rudest awakening of all! I'm not saying that body shape isn't important for feeling attractive. I'm saying that body shape is an individual feeling.

Whether you're slim or overweight or fluctuate between the two, the most important decision you could ever make regarding your lovability doesn't relate to what the mirror says, but more to how you interpret it. Sure, if being slimmer can help make you feel more attractive to others, make that the goal and take the action.

3. Keep a food diary

There are hundreds of different approaches to food and health. It can be paralysing trying to know what to eat for optimal happiness. The key here is to remain conscious of the signals coming from your body in the present moment, and if you *know* deep down that a food doesn't agree with you, have the strength to say 'no' to eating it.

You're the only person who gets to live in that body of yours, and if people think it's stupid, weird or daft to eat the new way you're eating, accept their need to be right and carry on living your way regardless. The present moment continuously offers you a myriad of sensations in each corner of your body, and it's your job to remain attuned to those signals so you can know what's best for your body.

Tips from your coach

- Keep a 'that DID NOT work' food diary. Logging everything you eat is a huge task, so what I advise people to do is simply jot down what definitely *didn't* agree with their body. In this way, you can keep track of what you need to keep out to stay on top form.

- If you visit friends and they serve something you can't or don't want to eat or drink, stay conscious with the love of your spirit – a spirit that *knows* exactly what it wants from life and why. Go to your heart and you'll find the right solution to any social/foodie situations that may come up.

4. Use the scale up, scale down rule

If you've been getting in lots of rest and food recently, scale down your eating and scale up your exercise. If you've not been eating much and doing lots of exercise, scale down your movement and scale up your rest and food. How do you know when you're in the right spot? Your body will tell you in the present. Just keep listening to it.

For example, if you're feeling sluggish and tired, it could be a good idea to listen to the cues and say 'no' to drinks with friends that night. If you're feeling restless or slightly anxious, it could be time to get a big workout in, instead of filing those papers when you get home. Each new moment is a moment to make a decision about what's optimal for your body and happiness.

How do you stay mindful of what your body needs? By doing your 10-minute morning meditation and mini-meding throughout the day. The more you meditate, the easier it becomes to be mindfully aware; and the more aware you are of your body, the easier it becomes to spot the signals.

The reverse is also true – let's say you have the signal from your body for rest but miss it because you're on autopilot and continue working your body hard. The result can end up overwhelming your nervous system.

Your wellbeing and happiness is a delicate balance. Even the slightest tip on those scales and you can lose control of it. It goes without saying you can never have perfect control over balance, but the scale up, scale down rule is a way of checking in with yourself in any given moment so you can keep on top of your energy and wellbeing levels.

5. Leave the future where it belongs

Recently, while travelling home on a crowded bus from work, I experienced a neat little example of present-moment wisdom relating to health. Sitting in front of me were two elderly gentlemen, one of whom turned to his pal and said, 'I'd love to eat how you eat, Bob, but I just don't have the discipline and it would make me so grumpy to eat that way. I mean, I'd love to improve my health, but it's just not sustainable for me.'

Bob replied, 'Mate, honestly, I have no idea what my diet will do for me long-term. I could die tomorrow and wouldn't know whether living this way had helped or not. But I know this much: when I eat this way, I feel good now. That's the only gauge we'll ever have, isn't it?'

Applying the Happiness GAP recap

I've worked with super-slim people whose inner confidence and overall happiness were low. I've also worked with overweight people whose inner confidence and overall happiness were high. The equation slim =

happy and confident is a myth. But among our sweeping generalizations, there are some grains of truth: the better we take care of our body through early nights, good nutrition and exercise, the better we'll feel, and the better we feel, the more likely we are to want to keep replicating that.

If you've had an up-and-down relationship with either the health or appearance of your body, some upward wellbeing spiralling might be a good move for you. It's as if, the moment we see even a *slight* result, this spark of inspiration can act as the catalyst for further change. Whether you're looking for that spark or just want to continue that upward spiral, ask yourself these questions:

▶ 'What am I grateful for in my body right now?'

▶ 'What do I need to accept as outside and inside my control right now?'

▶ 'Am I here, present with my body, my food, my life?'

Because, regardless of what the future holds for you and your beautiful bottom, checking in with yourself will continue to be the wisest move of all.

Happiness GAP case study

Lorraine (worried, and happier)

Lorraine was a dear woman who gave out a generous, warm energy. I thoroughly enjoyed spending time with her in our sessions – she was one of those people who's kind to the bone, and she taught me why it's in giving that we receive.

On top of her full-time job as the manager of a gym, Lorraine would do up to 30 hours of care for her terminally ill mother, while also helping the numerous friends who sought her phone-based counsel in the evenings.

Although Lorraine's goal was to have a tummy-to-butt ratio like Kylie Minogue's within six weeks, as our relationship and rapport grew, her 'real' goal revealed itself. As a teenager, she'd suffered from a lack of self-esteem and anxiety over how she saw herself, and this had passed on into adulthood. She'd always carried a bit of extra weight and, as she described it, 'It just feels like everyone's judging me all the time.'

To my surprise, Lorraine explained that she'd never had a positive thought or feeling about the way she looked or who she was. Why was I surprised? Well, not only was she kind to everyone she met, she also had beautiful features and great skin tone.

As the trust between us grew, Lorraine began to open up to me a little more about her feelings towards herself. During one session, she told me the kind of remarks she'd make in her mind: Urrggghhh – look at you. No one's gonna love you like this, you ugly blob!

To look at Lorraine, you'd assume she had men dropping at her feet, but once you got to know her, the difficulties she'd had with men made complete sense. She was giving off a don't-come-near-me vibe – not because she didn't want guys near her, but more because she didn't want to be near herself!

Lorraine took on the challenge of filling the Happiness GAP with open arms. Once she began strengthening her gratitude muscle, something cool started to happen: she was paying more attention to the positives in her appearance for the first time in her life. It didn't happen overnight, but around week three, she wrote this in her journal:

'I know I don't have the skinniest legs, but when I was in town today, I saw a lady with red marks all down her legs who wasn't shy about getting them out in public. I was so grateful for what she taught me about letting go of perfection and just letting myself 'be'.

'I have awesome legs, partly because my skin tone is nice, but mainly because they're mine. They're the only ones I'll ever have; they get me from a to b and, by God, I'd better start enjoying the bloody things before I'm a wrinkly old lady!'

In moments of weakness, Lorraine slipped back into old patterns about how she saw herself, and although she was slowly becoming more positive, she was still beating herself up with her own thoughts. Much as she'd done with the gratitude exercises, I urged her to be patient and simply pay closer attention to how her thoughts felt, looked and sounded.

Once she could spot the thoughts that weren't helping her, Lorraine 'reframed' them, using self-acceptance affirmations to unblock her emotional river. She went from an inner dialogue of I'm horrible and ugly *to* It's OK to be imperfect. I'm OK as I am.

Self-acceptance didn't solve Lorraine's problems entirely, but she was becoming easier on herself. She was much less on edge. My favourite of her affirmations was, 'I'm loving myself too much to want to feel bad about the way I look.'

Part of Lorraine's 21-day GAP challenge was to become more present with the moments she felt at her least confident, to see if there were any habits that were increasing her lack of self-esteem.

In one session, she said, 'I've really noticed how many mirrors just don't flatter me, so I've taken down a few of them at home. I'm also more mindful of how the smallest of individual moments affect me – from avoiding certain guys at work to which foods make me feel better. My mind is now so much sharper to what does and doesn't work for me.'

Lorraine used mindful awareness of the present moment to tune into her own true feelings – her intuition. It was amazing to watch her transformation: she was smiling more, making jokes and getting out and about to meet guys.

The GAP in action

G: *Lorraine's body-image gratitude muscle had become stronger, enabling her to see more of the positives in her appearance.*

A: *By tapping into a higher awareness of her thinking, she was able to notice when a thought was making her feel bad and instead just accept herself more.*

P: *Lorraine's mindfulness of the present moment helped her ride the waves of life with more ease, control and calm. By engaging with her spirit once in the morning and three times a day with a two-minute mini-med, she was able to reconnect with the calm/quiet/observing soul inside.*

CONCLUSION

Some Final Words from Your Coach

When I was 16, I worked as a cashier in a supermarket, and I loved it. On my first day, I was trained in how to operate the till. As diligently as my teenage self tried to focus on what my manager was telling me, my mind was on more important things, like whether to drink a strawberry or a banana protein shake in my mid-morning break.

After a week on the tills, I was having a fabulous time – chatting to customers, scanning items, giving cashback (so people didn't have to go to a cash machine) and joking about with the other staff.

However, around week three of my new job, things started to go a bit weird. One day, the head manager, Neil, asked everybody to stay back at the end of their shift so he could 'talk about something'. I was feeling a little sheepish (I was normally in trouble for something!), as Neil announced that there was *lots* of cash going missing from the tills during the day.

Next, we had to strip down to our pants and submit to a full body scan to make sure we were all telling the truth. The daily searches went on for a number of weeks, until one fateful Saturday afternoon. It was extra busy so I was asked to work on the stand-up till. I stood next to a colleague who was serving a customer when he asked for cashback. No big deal, but what caught my eye next took my light stomach to a sinking one.

As I watched the cashier press an extra two buttons to create a cashback transaction, I realized that I'd been doing it wrong the entire time and therefore had been giving people *lots* of cash, for FREE! I don't want to say how much it could have been, but let's just say it could have paid for a *very* nice car!

About an hour after I'd noticed the horrendous mistake I'd made, miraculously, we stopped being searched! Although my novice error cost the supermarket some serious wedge, looking back, the insight that pops up when I look back at the incident is how quickly I forgave myself for it.

Live each day like it might be your last

Where does that carefree inner child go as we become adults? That inner child with such lightness it's able to shrug off a mistake in minutes and move on? Well, nowhere really. It lies within us if we're willing to drop the baggage that weighs us down by taking ourselves and our lives too seriously.

We rarely see that childlike spirit in adults, but when we do, it's inspiring. These people light up a room and make others feel good. They travel light and they're happy. And in a funny kind of way, it's as if unhappy people act like they're going to live forever and happy people act like today could be their last – with childlike enthusiasm and light- heartedness.

I recently saw this spark in US surfer Gerry Lopez. While being interviewed before heading out into gigantic waves for the first time ever, he said casually, 'Well, dying today would be as good a day as any other, I suppose.' Or how about the comedy legend Spike Milligan, whose headstone bears the words 'I told you I was ill.'

I'm not telling you these little anecdotes because I want you to do the things concerned. I'm relaying them because I want you to live on what the writer and thinker Carlos Castaneda called 'the active side of infinity' – a level of awareness that acknowledges the ultimate truth about our physical lives on Earth: that every alive thing will have its date with forever.

So, why do we hold so much back in life when we're all going the same way? In my view, it's fairly obvious: our dying kinda stunts the progression of our species. In a wild world millions of years ago, we survived as a race because we were able to sniff out danger. The trouble is, life isn't like that any more. It's pretty darn safe and full of incredible opportunities. Opportunities for all of us? Yes! If we stop taking ourselves so goddamn seriously!

I mean, really? The ego's so precious that it wouldn't at least try and make a go of cutting coconuts? The soul is far too interested in expanding to care about inevitable bends in the road. All those times you were afraid that things wouldn't go to plan, of what might happen, of what people might think, tend to wash away when you meditate on the idea of your own death.

That's because doing so connects the reality of being here in the physical world with the Universal Mind: the part of you that observes life from a higher level of love, childlike spirit and ever-expanding consciousness.

And don't even get me started on whether we are worthy. Take a pause and think about this: US writer and personal growth consultant Dr Ali Binazir has calculated the probability of you existing as you today as one in $10^{2,685,000}$. That's a 10 with more that 2 million zeros behind it.

I mean, imagine this: if, a million years ago, Bob (your hairy male ancestor) hadn't taken a left at the mangrove swamp he might never have met Sue (your hairy female ancestor) for a hairy kiss by the water's edge. What if he'd taken a right? He'd have met Glenda, with a much less pretty mane of hair but an equally round bottom, and the person that is sitting here reading these words would never have come to be.

And consider this: YOU happened to be in the round of sperm in Dad, who instead of his usual Tuesday night beer with the guys, decided to turn it into a lovemaking one with Mum. Out of the other 50 million sperm, YOU won the race! Doesn't all this make you wonder how someone could ever question his or her worth?

I guess it comes back to a choice: we can ignore the fact we're going to die – in a vain attempt to be at peace with sweeping all of our creative, loving and inspired faculties under the rug of being unworthy – or remind ourselves to stop taking the ego so seriously and unleash everything we've got onto the dance floor of life.

Will you end up creating the life of your dreams one day? Who knows? And does it really matter to anything but your ego? Of course, we all want cool things to happen in life, but that's not why you have what it takes to become inspired. You have what it takes because 99 per cent of what you fear about life *will never come true.*

And the 1 per cent that could? You've already proven on thousands of occasions that you have more resilience to handle the outcomes than you give yourself credit for. Take a deep breath, look up at the sky, smile and feel that deeper trust return to your spirit. A trust and faith that's always there, in your soul, waiting like an old friend with open arms and a hug.

Surfing life's waves

On a surf holiday in Tenerife I got chatting with a local about the endless search for perfect waves. 'Waves are too crowded these days to have fun,' he remarked.

'Yeah?' I replied. 'I reckon people have been saying that since surfing started! It's only now that you're older and crustier that you're saying this. When you were a kid, I bet you never looked at it that way!'

'No, no!! It's genuinely more crowded now,' the guy insisted. 'If you wanna surf perfect waves, you've got to surf with so many other people, it sucks. I never seem to get the waves I want – other surfers keep getting in the way. The boards are too expensive these days, too. And my girlfriend constantly complains and bitches at me when I've been out in the ocean for too long!'

'Ahhh, you never said anything about the waves or surfing being perfect,' I said. 'You can always find less crowded waves and surf sessions if you accept they won't be perfect. Good enough for some fun though. Isn't the mere fact that we're surfing good enough, my friend? Isn't that enough to be thankful for?'

'Yeah, but I can't lower my expectations,' he replied. 'I'm too hungry for perfection.' To which I said, 'Well, you might just have to live with being the unhappy surfer' (after which there was lots of banter and laughing).

My hope is that by filling your Happiness GAP, you'll feel more accepting of those less-than-perfect waves you get to ride in your day-to-day; more thankful for being out there in the first place and present with whatever waves come your way in the surf. If you ever feel as if your life is taking a backward step, you can take the GAP programme again to re-establish happiness.

Having *full* control over where your future is going is like trying to control which wave comes your way in the surf. Sure, being in the ocean is a good start. But once you're in it, so much of what happens isn't down to you. Out of all the waves breaking on the shore, not a single one is the same as the last.

If you find yourself on a powerful wave, be present and enjoy the ride. If you find yourself on a slow one, don't wish to be off it. You can still enjoy the ride, as long as you don't wish you were on a faster one. As surf champion Phil Edwards once said, 'The best surfer out there is the one having the most fun.'

I know life can be tough sometimes, but I believe you have what it takes to get stronger, grow and be more. How do I know this when I don't even know you? Because inside of you is the ability to *choose how you want to think*. In a single moment, the entire course of your life can take a whole new direction. Never forget that! Take a single thought of hopelessness and change the picture to one of hope – then watch what happens!

Mother Nature didn't give you a mind so you could squander it on thinking small – she gave you the capacity to go big on this! Get out in that ocean, choose which waves you want to ride, and surf life *your* way. The sun is rising on the horizon, my friend: we've been on a cracking ride and thank you for reading this book. I hope I can meet you one day and share in your journey.

Much love,
Will x

Bibliography

The following books helped bring *Filling the Happiness GAP* into form:

The Pursuit of Perfect, Tal Ben-Shahar (McGraw Hill, 2009)

Happier, Tal Ben-Shahar (McGraw-Hill Education, 2008)

The Power of Intention, Dr Wayne W. Dyer (Hay House, 2004)

The Active Side of Infinity, Carlos Castaneda (Harper Perennial, 2000)

Just Get on with It, Ali Campbell (Hay House, 2015)

Effortless Success (audio CD), Michael Neill (Hay House, 2011)

The Seven Spiritual Laws of Success, Deepak Chopra (Bantam Press, 1996)

Big Magic, Elizabeth Gilbert (Bloomsbury, 2016)

The War of Art, Stephen Pressfield (Black Irish Entertainment, 2012)

The Gratitude Diaries, Janice Kaplan (Yellow Kite, 2016)

The Happiness Project, Gretchen Rubin (Harper Collins, 2011)

Mindfulness, Mark Williams and Danny Penman (Piatkus, 2011)

The Happiness Advantage, Shawn Achor (Virgin Books, 2011)

The Power of Now, Eckhart Tolle (Hodder & Stoughton, 2001)

Long Walk to Freedom, Nelson Mandela (Abacus, 1995)

How to Eat, Move and Be Healthy, Paul Chek (C.H.E.K Institute, 2004)

Perfect Health Diet, Paul Jaminet (Scribner Book Company, 2013)

Don't Sweat the Small Stuff, Richard Carlson (Hodder, 1998)

Face the Fear and Do It Anyway, Susan Jeffers (Vermilion, 2007)

Force of Nature, Laird Hamilton (Rodale Books, 2010)

The Secret, Rhonda Byrne (Simon & Schuster, 2006)

Daring Greatly, Brené Brown (Penguin Life, 2015)

The Art of Asking, Amanda Palmer (Piatkus, 2014)

The Happiness Hypothesis, Jonathan Haidt (Arrow, 2007)

Think and Grow Rich, Napoleon Hill (The Ralston Society, 1937)

ABOUT THE AUTHOR

Will Foster

Will Foster is a life coach and happiness expert whose work has been featured on ITV's *Lorraine*. He has personally trained and coached over 12,000 one-on-one sessions in the last 12 years, helping clients to understand who they are and what they want from their life. He has also spoken across Europe on the benefits of mindfulness and wellbeing.

Will's inspiring and fun-loving approach focuses on teaching people how to unearth their deepest values, act upon them, achieve more contentment for the moment and create more excitement for the future. He guides people to their truest potential, both personally and professionally, by overcoming fear of failure, rejection and not being 'enough', and empowers them to dare greatly, love deeply and live freely!

Will lives by the sea and is happiest in the middle of the ocean with big waves breaking around his surfboard, thrashing rain pouring on his head and a mix of sea lions and friends for company. He loves nothing more than to score a dawny surf, come home to his daughter, wife and spaniel for brunch, and chill in the garden listening to music.

 facebook.com/groups/willswellnesswarriors

www.willfosterhappinesscoach.com

HAY HOUSE

Look within

Join the conversation about latest products,
events, exclusive offers and more.

f   Hay House UK

   @HayHouseUK

   @hayhouseuk

   healyourlife.com

We'd love to hear from you!